JOY A. SCHULENBURG

Gay Parenting

ANCHOR BOOKS
ANCHOR PRESS/DOUBLEDAY
GARDEN CITY, NEW YORK
1985

ISBN: 0-385-19317-3

Printed in the United States of America
First edition

Library of Congress Cataloging in Publication Data

Schulenburg, Joy A.
Gay parenting.

Bibliography: p. 160
Includes index.
1. Children of homosexual parents—United States.
2. Homosexual parents—United States. 3. Custody of children—United States. 4. Lesbian mothers—United States. I. Title.
HQ777.8.S38 1985 646.7'8 85-6741

FOR MY FAMILY:
GEOFFREY, BERT AND VERONICA

ACKNOWLEDGMENTS

I would like to thank Patrick Brian Smith, M.S.W., for the many hours of research which he has contributed, and for his unflagging support, without which this book could not have been written.

Additionally, I wish to thank the following individuals and organizations for their assistance and for providing essential information: the Loving Brotherhood, Bay Area Physicians for Human Rights, Parents and Friends of Lesbians and Gays, Llana Lloyd and Children of Gays, National Gay Fathers' Coalition, Lesbian Rights Project, Greg Day of the Larkin Street Youth Center, Dr. David Matteson, Gay and Married Men's Association, Dr. Brian Miller, the Shanti Project, Randy Burns of Gay American Indians, the National Gay Task Force, Ron Wright and the Gay People's Parenting Group, the Gay Pride Foundation, the Lyon-Martin Clinic, Bay Area Gay Fathers, the Northern California Sperm Bank, Richard M. Godlove III and Wages Due Lesbians.

And, to the hundreds of individuals who shared their personal experiences with me, a very special thank-you.

CONTENTS

Gay Parenting

ONE

In Search of Support

This book evolved out of a personal need. When my daughter was conceived in 1980, I thought I was something of a freak—the only lesbian I knew who had deliberately chosen to have a child. I knew a few lesbian mothers but all of them had had their children prior to coming out, during a time in their lives when they considered themselves "straight." My two male coparents were in the same position. We all knew openly gay men who expressed a longing for children, but none of them had ever done anything about it. We could only assume that our situation (a long, close friendship culminating in a decision to have a baby and raise it together) was unique in the gay subculture in which we moved.

With no social guidelines we had to make up our own rules as we went along. Legalities, finances, the balance of power—all of these presented a creative challenge to our triad. We made a lot of mistakes in the first two years; if we had not been building on a friendship of a decade's duration, we probably would have made even more serious ones. Somehow we managed to persevere.

While I was pregnant, I experienced a strange sense of being invisible in the lesbian community. The more my tummy grew, the harder it was to strike up conversations with new people. I was puzzled by this and a little hurt until the day I walked into a women's establishment and someone came up to me and said, "Excuse me, this place is for lesbians." "Yes, I know," I told her and was rewarded by a pointed look at my burgeoning belly. It dawned on me then: motherhood is so intimately linked with heterosexuality in people's minds that they couldn't possibly see me as a lesbian. Who ever heard of a pregnant dyke?

Geof and Bert, on the other hand, weren't experiencing any culture shock yet—at least not publicly. Since they didn't have any physical signs of impending parenthood, none of the gay men they met knew about it unless they chose to tell them. They reported that most of these reacted very positively, considering the news exciting if a bit unorthodox.

The books I was reading to prepare myself weren't much help either. We decided to have the baby at home and so most of the childbirth books I accumulated had a fairly liberal tone. Still, every one I picked up was based on the premise that the parents would be one heterosexual woman and her heterosexual husband. All the prenatal and postpartum advice, all the child-development material, was centered around that traditional model. The greatest deviation from heterosexual coupledom that those childbirth sources presented was the profile of a single mother who was being coached by a woman friend. There was nothing that even came close to our real-life situation.

We were fortunate enough to find a natural-childbirth class that accepted both of the guys. It was a small, private class and the other expectant parents were all very nice but, from the start, we could see people looking at us, trying to figure out what our story was. By the time the five classes ended, they all knew. By and large everyone took it well, but it was in that class that I heard, for the first time, a question which has since been often repeated: "What about your child? Won't it be traumatic to have gay parents?"

Frankly, I don't think any of us had given this much thought (I said we made some mistakes). We were still absorbing the implications of parenthood for ourselves—as people first and as gay people second. All three of us had been out since our early teens, were comfortable, even casual about our orientation and open with our families. Furthermore, we live in San Francisco, one of the gayest cities in the world. We simply weren't used to thinking in terms of prejudice and oppression. In a sense, we had been living charmed lives, a fact that I wasn't to fully appreciate until I started this book and began talking to the lesbians and gay men across the country for whom oppression was a part of daily life.

The more our straight friends and relatives began asking questions (Won't you be socially handicapping your child? Are gays stable enough to be good parents? Do you think your child will be gay too? Can the courts take your kid away if they find out you're gay?), the more I realized that I had been shortsighted. Sure, I thought my baby, growing up in a gay household, would avoid social stigmas and have whatever sexual orientation was natural for him or her. I felt confident that (regardless of being gay or straight), I was stable enough as a person to be a very good mother and why would anyone take a child away from a good parent? But after the twentieth repetition of certain concerns, I began to wonder if I wasn't being overly optimistic. I resolved to find out more about other lesbian and gay parents and about their children.

It wasn't as easy as I thought. A search of gay bookstores turned up a few pamphlets, three books and a mimeographed bibliography that listed mostly Ph.D. dissertations and articles in obscure psychiatric journals. I was referred to a couple of support groups for lesbian mothers and gay fathers. Methodically working my way through these, I accumulated other references, chapters of books, legal manuals and case briefs. Some of it was trifling, some barely decipherable to the layperson and some simply outdated. There was good stuff too, research papers, a packet from the National Gay Task Force, articles written with knowledge and passion. It became clear very early on, however, that everything written was written to cover a specific aspect of parenting—custody, insemination, etc.—and everything was gender-oriented, either about lesbian mothers *or* gay fathers.

Granted, some issues are more sex-specific than others, but the common thread of discrimination is very strong. Owing to a number of factors (some of them still puzzling to me), no one had ever put together a resource that could be used by both lesbians and gay men involved with or interested in parenting. And no one had thought of including the parents' lovers and children. I sought out other gay parents and talked to booksellers, and each time the reply was, "No, there isn't such a book, but I wish there were." In the end, I determined to compile such a resource. You are holding the result in your hands.

I began work in December 1982 with a bare outline of subjects I felt needed to be covered. These were expanded as my knowledge and experience increased and I got a better handle on the issues that gay-parented families grapple with.

The first thing I discovered was how unusual my personal experience is. I have identified myself as a lesbian since the age of fourteen. From the beginning, I have had a supportive peer group and have experienced remarkably little prejudice or pressure to conform to a heterosexual role. As an adult, I chose to have a child and to share that responsibility with the two gay men who are my closest friends. The four of us (Bert, Geof, daughter Veronica and I) live together as a family unit and are accepted as such by our friends and families.

On the other hand, the great majority of gay and lesbian parents either did not recognize or did not accept their homosexuality until they were already married and had children. Their experience of parenting has been strongly colored by the coming-out process and the reactions of their families and associates. They have had to grapple with the legal system as well as their own attitudes.

Even among the increasing numbers of gay men and lesbians who are choosing to become parents after coming out, male and female coparents do not necessarily choose to live together as a family unit. Three-parent families are rarer still. I quickly learned to recognize my situation for what it is: a small minority within a minority group. Therefore, in order to produce a resource that would be relevant to the majority of gay parents, it was necessary to look well beyond my personal experience.

In an effort to draw a statistical sample from as wide a segment of the population as possible, I placed notices in gay and lesbian publications nationwide, asking for volunteers to complete questionnaires and be interviewed. This generated over five hundred separate pieces of correspondence. The information came from small towns, big cities, rural farms and foreign countries as people wrote, glad to find, some for the first time, a willing listener. Their tales reflect a rainbow of experiences, some happy, some tragic, some funny and some pure triumph over a world of misinformation and prejudice. All reflect a common theme: that lesbians and gay men are and have been loving, committed and effective parents able to raise secure and healthy children. These letters, and personal conversations with an additional two hundred parents, comprise the heart of the book. From the completed questionnaires I compiled some general statistics.

Forty-one percent of the respondents live in the Pacific region (including Alaska and Hawaii), 26 percent are in the Midwest and 15 percent reside in the Eastern states bordered by Washington, D.C., to the south and Ohio to the west. The remaining 18 percent are scattered throughout the United States and its territories. They represent a wide spectrum of philosophies and parenting styles. They average 2.1 children apiece—a figure so close to the American norm as to make them statistically indistinguishable from straight parents in this respect.

Regarding race, I find that the sample is rather uneven—probably due to some flaw in my distribution network. An overwhelming majority of those who completed questionnaires were white, although the parents I spoke with personally comprise a racial and ethnic mixture proportional to the population at large. The verbal material presented is, therefore, representative of a cultural diversity somewhat lacking in the statistical material.

The exact racial breakdown was as follows: 92 percent white; 2 percent black; 1 percent Asian; 1 percent Hispanic; 4 percent Native American. This last figure illustrates the vagaries of voluntary surveys. While, overall, only 30 percent of the questionnaires I sent out were completed and returned, I got back *all* of those distributed through a support group for gay Native Americans. I can find no evidence that there is a greater incidence of homosexuality among members of this group (although there is some historical precedence for a humane and sophisticated *acceptance* of gays in Native American culture). Rather, it appears to reflect a spirit of cooperation on the part of the individual respondents and a concern that this survey reflect the input of a too often ignored minority.

On top of the usual homophobia and misinformation, nonwhite gay parents often have additional barriers raised against them. Culturally induced poverty and racial prejudice within the legal system were those mentioned most frequently, particularly among women. I regret that I was not able to give specific minority concerns the in-depth study they deserve within the scope of this book, which is designed to cover issues common to gay parents in all segments of the population.

Ultimately, those issues fell into one of three general categories: *social and emotional concerns* (a wide-ranging category that includes coming out to your children, integrating lovers into a family unit, children's concerns, community attitudes, etc.); *legal implications* of homosexuality in child custody, adoption and artificial insemination; and *options* (the ways gay men and lesbians become parents). Some topics fall clearly within one of these categories. Most however, are a natural synthesis of all three elements that defy arbitrary division. They are presented in the context of personal experiences and in the words of individuals who have themselves confronted the different aspects of these issues.

I don't claim to have covered every subject with the fullness it deserves. There are too many issues here and there is too little conclusive research at this time. I have tried to present the basic information about these matters, to give voice to the millions of persons affected by gay parenting, and to open up a dialogue on the myriad issues that affect us. With so many points of view coexisting in this country, the political ramifications alone could make up a hefty volume. It is my intention to provide a resource, not to stir up controversy within the gay and lesbian communities. Where it seemed applicable, I attempted to address both men and women; where the issues are gender-specific they are so treated.

Some separatists may be offended by this approach but the majority of us do not live in a separatist world. I have attempted wherever possible to use pronouns and descriptives which are not gender-specific. While this may seem awkward to those used to our sexist language structures, I think it is a necessary step in breaking the barriers of thought and habit that limit us all.

More than anything else, this is a book about people. People who are gay and have children, young people whose parents are gay, people who share a part of their lives with gay-parented families. They are people of courage and concern. Many of them have risked scorn, prejudice and even physical danger to keep their families intact and then opened up their hearts and shared their experience so that others might learn from their triumphs and failures. They have taught me a tremendous amount about human love and endurance. Best of all, they have exemplified the qualities that are our community's greatest asset: diversity within the common bonds of dignity and freedom.

TWO

Between Two Worlds

Much has been made in both the gay and straight press of the so-called gay life-style. While the commentary on that style depends on whether the reporter's bias is homophobic or homophilic, the elements presented are fairly consistent and are often taken to represent the actuality of life for many gay persons and the aspirations of the rest. Whether the picture is painted with glitter and glamour or is one of sordid decadence, the overall effect has been to convince millions of people that gays live life in the fast lane.

The picture of the "gay life-style" is almost exclusively of men. Lesbians now and throughout history have been largely disregarded—a phenomenon of the patriarchal society that is, at best, a mixed blessing. The gays that the straight press tend to focus upon are the gay component of today's Young Urban Professionals, a vast consumer network of baby-boom children. They are young (twenty to forty-five) men living in a large metropolis with a sizable gay community, engaged in some professional occupation which ensures both social status and a healthy paycheck. Supporting only themselves, they are perceived to have a fair amount of disposable income which they spend pursuing the good things in life: tastefully furnished homes, clothes, regular workouts on Nautilus equipment, and enviable social lives including having readily available to them casual sex and recreational drugs.

A walk through San Francisco's Castro district, Chicago's New Town or New York's Greenwich Village confirms the existence of the gay urban professional. He is real; he is hot. He is the hallmark of the gay life-style purveyed in the discos, bars and a media that loves glamour spiced with risk. Dressed in a lumberjack shirt and forty-pound boots, he challenges the old stereotypes of the limp-wristed lisping queen or the middle-aged bachelor who tends his widowed mother and "just never met the right girl."

A few of the fathers interviewed for this book fit reasonably well into the mold but they are a minority. Overall, I saw almost as many different life-styles as parents.

Jim, thirty-eight, lives in a rural commune with his daughter Becky, age nine. His existence is a mixture of hard work, personal satisfaction and isolation from other gays. He has set out several times to explore the world and find support and substantiation for his homosexuality. Each time he has returned. "This is the only place I feel is safe to raise a child," he says of the commune's natural, self-sufficient environment.

Dorothy, twenty-nine, and Pam, thirty-two, share Pam's house in a Midwestern suburb. They also share the task of raising children—Pam's two daughters, aged eleven and nine, and Dorothy's son, who is eight. They have a station wagon, a motorcycle and a beat-up Chevy, four cats, three bedrooms and a babysitter on Saturday nights when they try to get into the city and socialize with other women. "We're just like most of the families in our neighborhood," they tell me. "Quiet, involved with the kids' schools and not inclined to make waves." While they do not go to any great lengths to hide their relationship, they have discovered that most of their neighbors are not inclined to question it either. They are out to a few friends and associates. "If they ask us, we'll tell them," Pam says shrugging. "But we don't ask about their sex lives; why should they ask about ours? I don't think anybody around here wonders. I don't know if they even care."

Tony is an airline executive. At forty-seven he is good-looking, even distinguished. He maintains platonic friendships with a few attractive women—acceptable dates for those social situations which his profession demands. His lover of three years has an adjoining condo which Tony helped finance. They both see other people from time to time and find the separate living arrangements convenient. Tony in particular prefers to have the second bedroom available when his teenage son comes to visit during the holidays. After nine years of divorce, his relationship with his son is primarily financial, generally polite but not especially warm. He feels that it is important for his career to promote his role as divorced father and is concerned that his son have an opportunity to grow up "normally." He has never considered having custody of the boy.

None of these individuals would fit comfortably into the others' environment. Each has evolved a life-style for very individualized reasons. In one instance, the parent put his child's well-being first, far above his own desire for contact with other gays. Perceiving the isolation of a rural setting as safest, he quite willingly chose it as the best place for their family of two. Other parents seek a middle ground, not perfect for nurturing either children or gay consciousness, yet allowing a little of both if carefully planned. Most of the parents we interviewed indicated that their life-style had evolved naturally, without a great deal of conscious planning. For some, jobs and career goals dictate much of the way they live their lives; for others family ties, availability of good schools or simple complacency were the deciding factors. Two things they did appear to have in common were concern for the child's physical and social well-being and a need for continuing contact with other gays. (Whether the needs were fulfilled is another matter.)

I looked at mothers and fathers, both custodial and noncustodial (including parents whose children were grown and gone), attempting to discover the common thread among them as well as the dissimilarities. Because of the nature of the study it is difficult to say if the trends seen are accurate representations of all gay and lesbian parents. The respondents were interested enough in the subject to voluntarily contact us to offer input; I can only assume that they represent "involved" parents, genuinely concerned with the issues at hand. Thus there was an inordinately large percentage of custodial parents in our sample as well as a large number who wanted custody but did not have it. Undoubtedly, there are also parents out there who are not particularly involved or interested in the issues of gay and lesbian parenting and whom I did not reach. Perhaps among them we would find those who fit more neatly into the media stereotypes; certainly the people we saw and spoke to shunned the mold.

In a society which tends to automatically grant custody to a child's natural mother, it is no surprise that more than three quarters of the women we contacted have custody or had it until their children were grown. Excluding the 10 percent of respondents who are married, that leaves fewer than 15 percent as noncustodial mothers in the sample, not enough to draw any conclusions regarding patterns in life-style. The most notable similarity between these women was bitterness: only one noncustodial mother had willingly given up custody of her children and that was to her own parents, whose environment and location was felt to be most beneficial to the children. Those who had lost custody of their kids reported depression (sometimes severe), guilt and a deep and abiding sense of loss.

The picture of the mothers with custody is one of hardworking women. More than any other group, these individuals tended to live in middle-class, suburban areas, particularly in the Midwest and California. Frequently they still live in homes or apartments established during a prior marriage. This is probably a reflection of traditional property settlements. Though precedents and laws are changing, it is still the norm for the woman to keep the kids and the house. Maintaining both in an adequate manner and staying afloat financially is often the challenge. Although a majority are entitled to child-support payments, it is not uncommon for an ex-spouse to forget or refuse those payments and threaten to expose the mother's lesbianism (or use it as a weapon to get custody) if she pursues legal channels to collect. Therefore, most lesbian mothers must support themselves and their children on one income—their own.

Although some of the mothers in our sample were professional women with prestigious jobs, the majority were barely making ends meet. Over two thirds of the female respondents indicated that they were nurses, secretaries, teachers or unskilled laborers, jobs which women traditionally perform for substandard wages.

There was somewhat more diversity among the gay fathers. A significant portion of them held graduate degrees in the fields of engineering, science and business administration. Others were employed as computer programmers, physiotherapists and photographers. Several were in or retired from the armed forces. The percentage of full-time parents was almost the same for men as for women; approximately 4 percent of both sexes described their occupation as "parent" or "homemaker."

While the divorced fathers had custody of their children less often than the divorced mothers, many of the fathers were quick to point out that they received child-support payments from their former spouses. Unlike the female respondents, however, these men did not indicate any difficulties in collecting monthly payments. This may be due, in part, to the fact that the men tended to have more amicable relationships with their ex-wives than the women had with their ex-husbands. I suspect it also has quite a bit to do with society's attitude, which assumes a mother's concern for her children's welfare even when they do not live with her. With very few exceptions, the children of custodial fathers maintained regular contact with their mothers. There is a clear-cut relationship between the involvement of noncustodial parents and the regularity of their child-support payments.

"One of the hardest things for me is that my friends who aren't parents don't realize that I don't have the amount of disposable income they do," says Doug, a noncustodial father who contributes substantially to his daughters' upbringing. "I'm not able to go out as often or spend as freely as they do and it makes me hesitate before agreeing to do something that could run into money. It's not that I don't like to have fun, but I can't always afford it!"

Doug's words were echoed by many of the parents we talked to. When we asked what advice they had for lesbians and gay men who were thinking about becoming parents, most of those who answered referred to the expense of raising children. "Think it over carefully," was one parent's advice. "Being a parent means investing a tremendous amount of your time and your money in your children. If you don't have some of both to spare, maybe you shouldn't have kids."

The current cost of raising a child is $135,000 from birth through age eighteen. That is a lot of money by anyone's standards. Of course, you do not have to have the entire sum up front in order to have a child. It is spent, bit by bit, month by month, over the years. Housing, food and clothing represent only a portion of the parent's financial contributions. There are medical expenses, childcare, entertainment costs, allowances, a million and one ways for the dollars to fly away. Like single heterosexual parents, lesbian and gay parents cannot count on a second family income to help offset the expenses of raising a child.

While budgetary constraints are one factor in distinguishing gay parents from their more stereotypical peers, an even more important factor is the presence of the children themselves. They are walking, breathing, loving reminders of our long-term responsibilities. Their dependence can limit, to some extent, the social opportunities enjoyed by our childless counterparts in the gay community. For the urban gay parent, raising children forces us to function in a heterosexual environment (schools, friends' parents, etc.) that we might otherwise choose to avoid. Despite the inconvenience, this is a task that most of us accept gladly for our children's sake. Unfortunately, our nonparent contemporaries don't always understand and gay parents find that they must make adjustments in gay environments as well as straight ones.

"I feel out of place in the gay community and I can't be myself in the straight world!"

Phrased in a hundred different ways, this statement came from dozens of gay parents, male and female. It is perhaps the major reason that gay parent support groups have sprung up in cities across the United States and Canada. Then, at least for the duration of a monthly meeting, the parents can sit down, talk with others like themselves and stop being outsiders.

Lesbian and gay parents are part of what has been called an

invisible minority. Unlike blacks, Asians or the disabled, it is almost impossible to single them out in a crowd or to locate them in the census records. Walking down the street with their children, gay men and lesbians vanish into the mainstream majority. Unless they are also walking arm in arm with a lover or wearing a lesbian pride T-shirt, everyone—gay or straight—assumes that they are heterosexual. Only they know that they are a part of a minority.

"It's frustrating," says Lorraine, who has two girls, five and seven. "When I'm with the kids I see the gay chauvinism that you hear about. That subliminal acknowledgment that gay people give one another in public simply isn't there. People see the kids and just assume I'm straight. They don't see me. And I don't identify with the straight community—but they see me as one of them and treat me accordingly. I can't relate to that, particularly to the assumption that I have a husband at home waiting for me. So most of the time I feel like a ghost, invisible whether or not I want to be."

Lorraine's dilemma is echoed by many of the parents I spoke to. Those who are just coming out in particular often feel a need to integrate themselves with the gay community, and that can be doubly difficult when there are children at home. The lesbian and gay social world is comprised largely of nonparents. The hassles of childcare, school pageants, teenage crushes and camp counselors are alien to these people. Being home in bed at a reasonable hour because a child has to be up at dawn never crosses their mind and the parent who makes an early night of it may be quite simply written off as a party pooper. As in the straight world, society can appear to be divided quite sharply between parents and nonparents with each group sticking to their own.

SUPPORT GROUPS: A COMMUNITY RESOURCE

Support groups have formed in cities and towns across the country for a wide variety of reasons. Some of the earliest were established to provide fund-raising drives and moral support for parents going through custody battles. Later, public education became a focus. Organizations such as the Lesbian Mothers Legal Defense Fund in Seattle, Washington, provide referrals, emotional understanding, encouragement and local contacts to those in need. In larger cities such as New York, the gay father may find that he has a choice of groups, each with its own unique structure and emphasis. One may be strictly a social club while another is active politically. Each of these groups serves to connect individual parents, provides a meeting ground so that the gay or lesbian parent need not face the unique dilemma alone.

In general, support groups for gay fathers are more structured and organized than the groups for lesbian mothers. The mothers' groups tend to be informal, encouraging emotional intimacy and psychological problem-solving. It is not uncommon for them to have begun as a couple of women with children getting together in someone's living room and growing strictly by word of mouth. The fathers' organizations, on the other hand, frequently structure themselves in a formal way, soliciting dues, electing chairmen, establishing a library and even incorporating. Many of them belong to the National Gay Fathers Coalition. Headquartered in New York City, this umbrella organization has dozens of local chapters. Their annual conference includes discussions and symposiums on a wide range of relevant topics, including lovers, children and coping with ex-wives, and draws hundreds of participants.

Parents and Friends of Lesbians and Gays is another national organization of support groups. Through media exposure (such as the "Dear Abby" advice column), this association has reached the families of gay people, helping them come to terms with homosexual relatives. A number of the parents I talked with had taken their parents and their children to at least one meeting, exposing them to nonhomophobic peers. The meetings provide families with a forum for discussing concerns and fears and a chance to be educated about common misconceptions.

Some of the parenting support groups have an auxiliary group for children of gay parents. While Mommy or Daddy is exchanging thoughts about parenting, the kids get a chance to socialize, understand and form friendships with others whose home life and concerns may be similar. Normally, few kids had peers with any real insight into their experience. Regular contact with other children of gays lets these kids know that they are not the only ones in the world with "different" parents.

Llana Lloyd, founder of Children of Gays, a Los Angeles–based organization, fields calls from across the country from children coming to terms with a parent's homosexuality. By her estimate, there are over six million children of lesbian and gay parents in North America. The satellite groups of her organization will help bring these people together for mutual understanding and support. Appearing on "Donohue," she brought the issue to national attention, using her own experience and stability to counter the homophobic assertion that children raised by gays turn out warped and neurotic.

"I'm always being asked if my mother's lesbianism stigmatized me," she reports. "People want to think that I didn't have any friends as a child because I was afraid to bring them home. That just isn't true." She considers a minute. "If anything, I had better friends than a lot of kids because I consciously chose people as friends who had open minds, who were not judgmental. It helped me to be a better judge of character. They also ask if I am a lesbian because my mother was one." She laughs and gestures to herself. Llana's appearance is what some people would call "ultrafeminine"—long blond hair, manicured nails, makeup. She turns men's heads as we walk through the lobby of her plush hotel and does not seem to mind it a bit. "I'm not a lesbian." She does maintain, however, that "you can't put people in boxes—straight, gay, bisexual, whatever. You have to take people as individuals, for their own worth. My mother is also one of my best friends. It has nothing to do with her sexuality, it's just the way she is. I'd like her if she weren't my mother, weren't a lesbian; why should I care for her any less because she *is* both of those things? She's a person. That's what I see."

All the evidence indicates that support groups, when they are available, provide the gay or lesbian parent with a vital link with his or her own identity. Here, meeting together, are others with the same set of concerns, the same priorities, the same needs and, sometimes, new solutions.

"My lesbian mothers group saved my sanity when I was going

through custody litigation," claims Adrienne, mother of two young boys. "Here were people who understood when I wanted to cry with frustration or scream with anger. They knew what I was going through because some of them had been there themselves. It helped me so much, seeing that they had survived all this. And it took the pressure off of my lover, Libby. She was trying so hard to be everything to me—friend, counselor, lover, coparent—and it took a big chunk of energy to do it. With the other moms to talk to about the parenting stuff, it gave us more time to just be together. She started being my lover again instead of my sounding board."

Other Influences: Who's Minding the Children?

Although support for a parent's gay identity can be found in one of the affinity groups, interaction with the straight community of schools, families and children's peers must be dealt with by individuals. We are not the only influence in our children's lives; before they are grown they receive input from a wide variety of sources.

While every parent is concerned about the people and situations that their child comes in contact with, gay parents are doubly cautious. Not only do they want to screen out the usual "bad" influences and dangerous individuals, they want to prevent the common cultural ingraining of homophobia, born of ignorance and fear. That this homophobia pervades almost every level of society and class makes the prevention no easier; some parents will go to great lengths to avoid it, choosing to raise their children in isolation or in a gay or lesbian commune environment. Most of us, however, desire to live our lives and raise our kids, as regular members of the larger society. We must, therefore, be prepared to face society's attitudes with strength and foresight, making the wisest choices we can.

With only 4 percent of the respondents listing themselves as "full-time parents," it is clear that the majority of lesbian and gay parents have to seek some outside childcare for their kids. This may be full-time day schools for small children or after-school care for school-age kids. Additionally, parents need babysitters for occasional nights out or those situations where it is not appropriate to bring the children along. Entrusting another person with the physical, emotional and psychological well-being of your child is nothing to take lightly. For the gay or lesbian parent, finding childcare that is responsible and nurturing is not quite enough: we want to make sure that the environment doesn't foster the homophobia so casually accepted by a heterosexual world. Some gay parents have solved the problem with a little work and forethought.

In most cases where the custodial parent had a lover relationship of any duration, the lover indicated that she or he participated in childcare to some extent. This ranged from covering for an hour or two on Saturday mornings while the parent went to a class, to providing full-time care for a very young child while the parent worked. Occasionally, the lover was also a parent and childcare responsibilities were split equally for the children of both with one parent working days, for example, while one worked nights. A few lovers were currently unemployed or had at-home jobs. They found it financially more reasonable to take on the childcare responsibilities themselves than to pay a stranger. This was most often true when the lovers held joint finances. At the very least, parents with lovers felt that they had someone to watch the children in emergencies—a reassuring situation. And, almost without exception, the children were pleased with the arrangement. Rather than having to mind a relative stranger in the impersonal setting of a daycare center or someone else's home, they had the comfort and security of their own surroundings and, oftentimes, the attention of one whom they felt to be another member of the family.

Throughout history, grandmothers have been providing a necessary source of childcare and nurturing. Though this supplementary care has been declining as more women of all ages enter the work force, it continues to account for a good deal of nonparent care and guidance. Recent studies comparing lesbian mothers with heterosexual single mothers show that both groups tend to rely on their families equally. That is to say, when the rapport with families (parents in particular) is good, both lesbian and straight mothers call on them for childcare, financial help and emotional support.

Of course, some concern arises about the influence of families when those families are felt to harbor homophobic attitudes. Some parents reported that their kids got subtle (or not so subtle) signals of disapproval regarding Mommy or Daddy's life-style. As one mother reported, "My mom used to ask Tommy, 'Does your mother have a boyfriend yet?' and Tommy would say, 'She doesn't need one, Gramma, we've got Cathy living with us.' So Grandma would frown and reply, 'That's just until she's ready to get married again.' I had to put a stop to that kind of propaganda by telling Mom that if she didn't quit it I'd find another babysitter. She was more concerned about spending time with Tommy than about my lesbianism, thank God. But it was a really tense situation for a while waiting to see what he'd come home with at night after being with his grandparents all day."

Some of the parents in the survey reported that there were periods of distancing from their families. This usually occurred during or just after the coming-out period. The good news is that these rifts are seldom permanent. After the initial shock wears off, most parents find that their children's and grandchildren's well-being matters far more to them than their bedroom activities. Their acceptance may be grudging or they may pretend that the subject of sexual orientation has never come up. Ultimately, however, the distance lessens; most grandparents want as much contact with their grandchildren as they can have.

Only a few of our respondents indicated that a member of their family provided full-time childcare (though in a few cases, the children actually lived with a grandparent). Parents and siblings were generally called upon to provide occasional weekend or evening babysitting, or perhaps a vacation during the summer months. Siblings frequently traded back and forth, babysitting for each other's kids. In this respect, there appears to be little difference between gay and straight parents. One interesting note was that lovers' parents and siblings frequently got involved with the kids. Several parents reported that their children regarded their partners' parents as another set of grandparents and that the elders spoiled, pampered and encouraged them with the same love and indulgence as blood relatives. Clearly such a situation could occur only when the parent and their lover were out to the grandparents and the relationship accepted as a legitimate bond.

For the parent who is out in most aspects of life, finding schools and daycare centers that are appropriate and not likely to foster homophobic attitudes can be a genuine challenge. Only careful screening and observation of the faculty prior to enrollment is likely to ease your mind. If there is something you question, check it out. If the staff's philosophy or attitude seems distasteful to you, go to another school; it is better to have to drive a little out of your way each day than to cope with negative attitudes picked up by kids in a homophobic environment.

If you are not at ease having your child's teacher or babysitter know you are gay, you may find it difficult to explain why your lover picks the kids up half the time or is involved enough to attend PTA meetings with you. In urban areas this is less likely to be questioned for there are so many varieties of "family" that another adult involved with your child won't arouse curiosity. Some women's centers in bigger cities run daycare centers where such problems don't exist but, for the average American, child-care options are limited. You may have to do some juggling, you may have to explain to your child that there are some things we simply don't discuss at school such as why Harold lives with you and Daddy and makes your lunch every day. Much will depend upon your child's ability to cope with questions and the prevailing attitudes in your community.

While concern and forethought are quite appropriate in choosing outside childcare and schools, the actual incidence of homophobic input on the part of teachers and staff (peers are something else) was minimal among the families I spoke with. Perhaps it is that very forethought and careful screening of facilities that makes this so. However, it appears that the children themselves often handled the situation with remarkable tact and circumspection, essentially screening their environment themselves. When faced with negative attitudes toward their parents, these kids showed where their allegiance lay—with the families who gave them a foundation of love and nurturing, regardless of sexual orientation.

THREE

Coming Out to Your Children

This one day when I was about sixteen, my dad came home and told us that he'd come out. I asked what did that mean and my brother said, "It means he's a fag." At first I thought it was a joke. I mean, he's just a regular guy like anybody else's father.

—DANIEL, age eighteen

In the vernacular of the lesbian and gay community, the term "coming out" has a variety of connotations, none of which is much related to debutants or cotillions. It refers to the varying degrees of recognizing, acting upon and accepting one's homosexual preference. A person "comes out" on a personal level by admitting and/or acting upon an attraction for a member of the same gender. Socially, coming out involves putting yourself in touch with other homosexuals through friendships, bars, organizations or any other context in which gays identify themselves to each other. Finally there is the experience of coming out to others who are, presumably, straight.

In a homophobic culture such as ours, coming out publicly can be a risky venture. Some gay activists insist that one is not truly "out" until she or he is able to say to anyone, anytime, "I am gay." Only by standing up and being counted, they say, can we show our true numbers and make changes. Well, they are right. And yet, for the majority of gay men and women, such public disclosure of private preference puts them in jeopardy of losing friends, jobs, family and, in the case of gay and lesbian parents, their children.

A woman correspondent in Kentucky writes that her parents were awarded custody of her fifteen-year-old son after it became known that she was involved in an intimate relationship with another woman. "The strain of it almost broke me." She is not alone. The sad thing is that both the grandparents and the judge truly believed that they were acting in her son's best interest, regardless of the feelings and wishes of both mother and child. Yet up until the revelation that their daughter was a lesbian, they had regarded her as a good mother. The only thing that changed was their knowledge of her sexual preference.

Fortunately, such occurrences appear to be decreasing as the public and the judicial system become more educated about the realities of homosexuality. Courts in several states have ruled that sexual orientation alone is insufficient reason to deny custody to a parent. (There are several loopholes here that will be discussed in Chapter Eleven.) Of the 20 percent of respondents who experienced custody problems directly related to their sexual orientation, more than half were able to retain full or joint custody of their children. This represents a vast improvement since the 1960s. Even so, if 10 percent of gay and lesbian parents have lost custody of their children solely because of their sexuality, the number of lives affected is in the hundreds of thousands.

Of more immediate concern to gay parents is their child's reaction to discovering that Mommy or Daddy is gay. They fear rejection, hostility or embarrassment, culminating in a less close relationship with the child. This concern rose up time and time again as correspondents shared their thoughts. While four out of every five parents have come out to their children, many of them struggled for years with the question of whether to "tell the kids," fearing that their children would not be able to cope with the information. A full 20 percent have not been able to approach the issue and many of those who have "told" admit that they have mentioned but not really discussed the matter in any depth.

What, then, is the reality surrounding parents' fears of disclosure? How do kids react when they are informed that Mom or Dad is gay?

The statistics compiled for this book show that most children's attitudes are positive ones. When asked how their kids felt about the parents' homosexuality, fewer than 10 percent indicated that their children were unhappy or resentful, while more than 30 percent said that the kids were happy and proud of their gay parents. The majority appeared to be indifferent to the knowledge (41 percent), as expressed in a comment made by one eleven-year-old that "as long as he's still my dad, I don't care about that other stuff." Kids, as any parent knows, are remarkably adaptable, able to assimilate and work with circumstances that would push an adult beyond his or her limits.

The question of whether or not to come out to your children automatically leads into the question of when. What is the best age to inform a child that her or his parent is gay? Very young, before opinions are formed and conditioning ingrained? Or later, when the child has his or her own sexual identity established?

On the basis of talks with parents and children of all ages, it appears that the first course is the most desirable. Parents and children both felt that it is better to tell a child when they are young than to risk having them find out from someone else in the wrong way. Many parents waited until they were confronted by a curious (read: suspicious) youngster. Such an approach can turn revelation into confession, an admission of some sort of guilt. This is particularly true when the child has already been allowed to accept society's negative biases against gays.

Negative conditioning appears to be pretty well established by the time a child is eleven or twelve and boys seem more susceptible than girls. In the era of women's liberation, girl children receive encouragement to be both flexible and strong, to analyze their options. Their mothers, particularly if they are lesbians, impart a sense of pride in strength, in fighting against the established order to achieve social equality. Boys, on the other hand, have not yet received all the benefits of liberation. While society is beginning to condone female strength (more at least than a decade ago), boys still are sent signals that they have to be tough, to be macho, to be "masculine." A gay father is not perceived as supporting traditional masculinity, nor is he breaking the status quo in an acceptable way.

More than one father of daughters has confided, "If I had boys instead of girls, I would have done things differently." Adam, a forty-four-year-old father of two teenage girls, says: "In terms of their need for a role model, I might not have been as open . . . If I had come out to an eleven-year-old son, I'm not sure I'd have taken him to Gay Pride Day like I take my girls . . . I might have played it straighter."

This should not be taken to mean that every daughter will accept it (though the overwhelming majority do), nor that all adolescent boys will react with hostility. Much depends on the existing relationship between parent and child. Says Earl, an educator and gay activist with two adult children: "I think the most difficult thing for parents is to deal with teenagers by treating them not as children and not as adults; they are adolescents. It's a time when kids are starting to have their own sexual wishes. Parents who are still insecure about their own sexuality may have problems with that." He came out to his own son when the boy was fourteen. "I said, 'When I was your age, I knew I could be either married, I could be a monk, or I could be gay,' and he said, 'Uggh! I could never be a monk!' "

Divorced when her children were nine and seven, Lucy had her first relationship with a woman a year later. Her sense of relief at having finally discovered the source of her differentness was profound; she was soon actively involved in several lesbian political and social groups. Yet for many years she kept her lesbian consciousness separated from her attitudes as a mother.

"I waited to tell my kids about my sexuality until they were in their teens, until I felt that they had their sexual identity established. Looking back, I can see that I was afraid that if they knew about my lesbianism, it would 'influence' their sexual choice! Which is ridiculous, since I don't feel that anyone, particularly not my mom, influenced me to become a lesbian; it's just the way I am. In a way, I copped to the very guilt that I am now fighting to eliminate. I would have felt guilty if one of my kids had been gay, and yet my influence as a mother is only partial. They have a straight father they're close to and, my god, the social influence to be straight is tremendous! Still, I was insecure enough to think that presenting lesbianism as a viable option (just one option, mind you!), would be contrary to my responsibility as a good parent."

And so she waited. Her eighteen-year-old son did not appear to react at all to the revelation, yet as time went by Lucy realized that he had begun to avoid her. He avoided bringing his friends around to the house, though at one time their family room had been filled with noisy teenagers. She tried to bring the subject up herself, wanting to clear the air, and was rebuffed at every turn by the statement "I don't wanna talk about it."

Her sixteen-year-old daughter was definitely uncomfortable but communicated rather better. "Her main concern," says Lucy, "was whether I was going to cut off my hair and start wearing men's clothing. Once I told her that nothing had changed or was going to change about my behavior she seemed to pretty much forget about it, except when something on the news or in the papers mentioned gay. Then she'd give me a look out of the corner of her eye. She started wearing more makeup and talking about boys more right about that time too, but whether she was compensating for me or it was just that time of her life, I'm not too sure."

Gay and lesbian parents like Lucy are up against a double dilemma: not only do they have to contend with society's homophobic attitudes influencing their children's judgment and expectations, they have to fight against their own antigay conditioning as well. Very few of us have managed to grow up gay in

America and not be affected by the general notion that homosexuality is "abnormal."

Any committed parent wants his or her child to be happy, to be stable. We worry about health and influences and making sure the kids get good role models. Staying out of trouble is not enough; we want our children to feel good about themselves, all the more if we have had to struggle against negative conditioning in order to accept and like ourselves—as people and as gay men and lesbians. We no longer have to accept society's judgment that we are "sick" or "unnatural" because we have an affectional preference for members of our own sex. Our children must live in this world too and our job is to prepare them for it. We hope to impart the best of ourselves to them and to give them the tools for overcoming the negative things they will encounter. This is a tall order, made more complicated by the fact that, as a minority, we automatically bestow minority status upon our children. Our kids cannot play ostrich. Like it or not, if they know that we are gay, they must, to some degree, confront the issues of homosexuality and judge those issues for themselves.

What is reassuring is that so many lesbians and gay men have raised happy, healthy children, despite the social pressures. When asked if they had any advice for other parents and would-be parents, those who had the most positive experiences were overwhelmingly emphatic about one thing: be comfortable with *yourself* as a person. Be secure in your own beliefs and accepting of your own sexuality and your children will be able to accept it also, for then they will be able to base their judgments on a positive model. Children learn their prejudices. If the parents are guilty and resentful over being gay, the children will assimilate that guilt and resentment. On the other hand, if the parents demonstrate pride, acceptance and security, those are the traits the child will emulate. Thousands of gay and lesbian parents are learning to pass on to their children a legacy of strength and pride.

Lindsay is one of the children who figured things out for herself. Now fifteen, she has lived in New York City with her gay father and in Oklahoma with her straight mother and so has witnessed a vast difference in attitude. She strikes one as an exceptionally poised and articulate young woman and yet, for all that, she seems much like any other bright, pretty teenager in her interests and goals.

I told my father when I was ten years old . . . we were sitting down to dinner, me and him and Bob, his lover, and I stopped eating and I looked up at him and I said, "Dad, are you gay?" and he said, "Yes, I thought you knew," because he thought that my mother had told me. And I turned to Bob and I said, "Does that mean you're gay too?" And he said "Yes," and I said, "Well, that's okay, I'm straight," and I kept on eating.

What made you ask that question?

Here I come from a small town in Oklahoma, where women and women don't hold hands, where men and men don't hold hands, where women kiss one another on the cheek but men, never . . . and I'd see friends come to my father's house and they'd greet each other with a little kiss and I thought that was kind of irregular, so finally, I asked.

Did you have any knowledge of what gay meant at the time?

Not really. When my father and Bob lived in Philadelphia and I was out there visiting one Christmas, I heard the word "gay" and asked them what it meant . . . Dad explained . . . so I understood. Actually, I just thought that they were roommates, friends, until I put two and two together. I would see it on Christopher Street, for example, because we lived near there, but Bob and my dad never touched . . . and they would not sit close to each other until I was about fourteen.

Do you think if you hadn't asked your dad, he would have told you?

No, he thought I knew, you see. He thought that my mother had told me, but she left that to him because it was "his problem," not hers. That was *my* problem. They never really made sure *I* understood because they never touched in front of me—except hug which I could see out here. But they never would touch so I didn't put it together.

Some parents have handled coming out to their children with tact and success and others seem to have botched the job, creating confusion and/or resentment. A few guidelines may be helpful in approaching the task. Obviously you will know your child and your situation best; not all of these will work for everyone. But the following have worked successfully for many people.

1. Come to terms with your own gayness first. This is the most important consideration. Parents who consistently demonstrated shame or confusion about their sexual identity consistently reported problems with negative reactions from their children. You set the precedent for acceptance and positive attitudes. If you need to sort out your own feelings on the subject, seek help from a counselor or support group.

2. Don't wait until your children know or suspect that you are gay to discuss it with them. Tell them as soon as you think they are old enough to understand, preferably before age twelve, when peer pressure and attitudes can overshadow parental input. The longer they are exposed to homophobia in society without any attempt on your part to counter it, the more difficulty they will have in understanding *you*. Don't let them hear it from friends or a hostile ex-spouse who may present homosexuality as a means to put you down.

3. Don't "confess"; inform. In other words, don't make a big deal out of it by overwhelming them with a revelation. Obviously you'll want to be ready, emotionally and psychologically, to deal with any reactions, but setting up a big confession scene only creates pressure for everyone. "I just thought that you should know that I'm gay. Since it's not something that everyone does or even approves of, I thought you should hear it from me so that you can understand that it's okay." Simple, casual presentations foster casual acceptance. Heavy "Sit down, son, I have something very important to tell you" scenes work better on TV soap operas than in real life.

4. Let your children know that this doesn't change your relationship or feelings for them. Reassure them that you are still exactly the same person you were yesterday and that your love for them is as strong as ever. This seems to be the biggest concern of younger kids. A lot of parents reported that children asked, "Are you still going to be my mommy/daddy?" Once assured that this was not an issue, the reply was generally, "Okay. That's all I care about." Let them know that gayness is just one aspect of you, like the color of your eyes or your taste in music—important, but not the only thing that defines the person you are. Put it into perspective.

5. Be prepared to answer questions. Unlike straight "birds-and-bees" sexuality, there are no cartoon picture books to explain gay relationships to small children. But there may be a few questions from kids who already have a grasp of what heterosexual relations are about. Things like "Does that mean that you kiss other guys?" or "Why can't you and Cheryl just get married, Mommy?" should be answered in a simple, straightforward way, without justifications or elaborate explanations that will only confuse. Kids whose parents are available and open to being questioned adjust better than kids whose parents simply inform them that they are gay and then shut the door on further discussion. If you can't deal with a particular question, try to find someone who can—perhaps your lover or a trusted friend or relative who has a good grasp of the issues. Make it a continuing dialogue so that as your child grows and learns new things about herself and society, she or he feels free to approach you for additional information.

6. Utilize available supports. If you are fortunate enough to live in an area where there are support groups for gay parents and their children, investigate them. Perhaps you don't feel that you need the interaction, but your child just might need or enjoy meeting other children in similar circumstances. Particularly for adolescents, peer support can make the difference between acceptance and confusion.

If there are no support groups you might consider giving your child one of the (admittedly few) children's books geared to children of gays. They are listed in the resource section of this book and can be ordered by mail if your local bookstore does not stock them. Even if your children are accepting of your gayness, they will probably enjoy reading these books. My own daughter, at three and a half, is particularly fond of *When Megan Went Away,* the story of a family coping with the breakup of the mother's lesbian relationship. Her comprehension of the story surprised me because the book was written for children in the six-to-ten-year-old bracket. It may be that she does not distinguish this yet as a gay story, but I like knowing that as she grows it will become part of her literary repertoire. Including such books in a child's library gives them role models and peers in an entertaining and positive context.

7. **Stay calm.** Let me repeat that I encountered very few children who totally rejected their parents solely because they were gay. Even kids who had an initially negative reaction eventually came to understand and even support their "different" parent. If coming out to your children appears to create negativity or antagonism, consider family counseling with a sympathetic therapist. It can provide everyone with a safe arena for discussion and letting off steam.

By and large, your own attitude about your sexuality and the emotional tone of your presentation will be the strongest influences on your child's level of acceptance. If you don't panic, neither will they. And if you remain open to resolving any conflicts, chances are that they will become active participants in a resolution. Simply being the best parent that you can, regardless of gender or orientation, helps foster the communication and trust that are so essential to coping with society and homophobia.

FOUR

The Children

Society's Fears and Their Own Concerns

Recently I told the director of my daughter's preschool that I was writing a book about gay and lesbian parenting. For a minute, she looked puzzled then asked,

"What do you know about gay parents?"

I was astounded by her question. From the day that we enrolled Roni in the school, I had thought that it was pretty clear that she had three gay parents—Mama, Papa and Daddy. Certainly we never made any attempts to disguise or avoid the subject.

"Everything," I replied, my surprise making me presumptuous.

"Oh." She blinked maybe once or twice then said, "Well, I hope the school gets a copy as soon as it's out."

"You'll be the first," I promised her and we went on to discuss my daughter, the discipline problem. Apparently my revelation (if it was that) hadn't made any difference in her attitude toward us or toward Roni. Yet for a few days I wondered, maybe even worried a bit in secret, that my boldness would cause my daughter to be treated differently—with scorn, pity or caution. Like a majority of lesbian and gay parents, I harbored a secret fear that my sexual identity might stigmatize my child.

In a questionnaire distributed to children under twelve, I asked, "Do any of your friends ever say anything about your parent being gay?" Only one child in several dozen replied, "Yes." "This kid said something about queers," wrote Jason, age nine. "I told him to shut up 'cause he didn't know anything and he shut up and never said anything again." The rest of the youngsters said that they received absolutely no feedback whatsoever. Half of them said that other people (family members, peers, teachers) knew that their parent is gay. The other half said either that no one knew or that they didn't know if anyone knew. In the under-twelve age group, not a single child reported being singled out and/or harassed because of a parent's sexual orientation. These included children whose parents were very much out in their community.

There have been cases in which a gay parent was denied custody of a child not because he or she was an "unfit" parent per se, but because of the "social stigma" the court *believed* the child would face. Many lawyers strongly advise their gay clients seeking custody or adoption to avoid anything that could be construed as gay activism, noting that courts take a dim view of "flaunting" a gay life-style. What this stigma is or how it manifests itself is yet to be proven; it appears to be a convenient excuse for homophobia.

Kate, a St. Louis mother of three daughters, was an activist for many years before she recognized her lesbianism. Denise, eighteen, recalls that her mother was "always talking to us about minority issues, as long as I can remember. There were all these books around and sometimes you'd get, well, sort of trapped into sitting and being read to for hours. We got a lecture on whatever she was into at the time. And there were always all kinds of people in our house visiting. Mom made sure to tell us, 'This one's gay' or 'He's a Buddhist' or whatever."

Renee, fourteen, nodded. "Yeah, there were lots of people. I didn't really see any difference for a long time." She is unsure exactly when her mother came out to her. Her sisters, who were both teenagers at the time, say that this occurred when Renee was nine.

"She was in women's studies," noted Kelly, twenty. "She had some lesbian-oriented books around. I remember that there was this woman who approached her at school and she came home and told us about it; she was really excited, but she wasn't out or anything yet. When she finally said something, it was like, very casually, 'You girls know I'm a lesbian, don't you?' and, by then it was like, oh; well, of course; I think I just said, 'Oh, *mother!*' "

I asked if they had felt any social prejudice against them. All three shook their heads no.

"There probably is," said Denise, "but I don't usually associate with those kinds of people—ones with closed minds."

"Right." Renee said. "I don't tell everyone because it's none of their business. But I don't lie about it either. If my friends want to know why my mother has these posters and things, I'll tell them, but I don't shout about it. Kelly's the one who likes to shock people."

"I do," Kelly agrees. "I like to spring it on people, especially people who are making fun of gays. It embarrasses them and maybe they'll think twice next time." I asked if there was a specific incident that she could recall and she nodded quickly. "My mother was on the news one time and this neighbor came over to tell me about my mom being a lesbian, like she thought it would surprise me. I surprised her though when I just said I know, when she thought she was going to get me or something. And I told this woman at work who was making gay jokes about my mother. It really shocked her that I would say it so easily. She didn't make any more jokes."

So, it would seem that the children of gays are educating people. The stigma so feared by nervous parents and courts alike was not apparent to most of the children I spoke with. Rather, I encountered frequent stories about embarrassed friends or coworkers who learned, after making some antigay remark, that their associate had a gay parent. The children were not being taunted or harassed.

Among the children I talked to and corresponded with, there were distinct differences in attitudes between those who had been under twelve when they learned their parent was gay and those who had been twelve and over. The under-twelve age group seemed largely indifferent to their parent's sexual orientation (which is true also of children of heterosexuals). Most of them simply didn't understand what all the fuss was about. Parents were loved because they were parents, despite any personal quirks and without reservations. Once puberty set in, with its sexual awakening and attending social pressures, reactions varied and the incidence of concern and initial rejection increased.

The children's initial concerns ran the gamut of misconceptions and homophobia, depending upon what they had already been taught about homosexuality. Only a few (usually those whose parent had expressed guilt and sought therapy in order to "go straight") feared that their parent was mentally ill, while nearly half initially wondered whether the mother or father was acting out of rejection of or by the opposite-sex parent. The more sophisticated, urban teens (who represented more than 70 percent of the over-twelve group surveyed) were worried about social or health matters: the possibility of a gay father contracting AIDS (addressed in Chapter Seven) or losing a job, community standing or religious sanction. Ninety percent of these said that time and experience had ultimately resolved their social concerns. The remaining 10 percent had either just found out that their parent was gay (within six months prior to the survey) or did not live with the gay parent in a close relationship.

While some of the parents told of children who had completely rejected them, avoiding all contact, a vast majority indicated that their children were either positive and accepting (31 percent) or indifferent (41 percent). Only 8 percent of the parents had children who were unhappy or openly hostile regarding their homosexuality. (Twenty percent of all the parents surveyed were so concerned about the possibility of rejection or loss of custody that they had not yet come out to their kids.)

Among the adolescents, one fear was predominant, even after social concerns were resolved: that of homosexuality being hereditary or contagious. One young man, the only one of three children who did *not* automatically reject his lesbian mother, confessed, "I used to lie awake at night and wonder if I'd turn out to be gay too." A number of other boys and girls echoed this concern.

"I know the scientists say it's not hereditary," said one teenage girl, "but how can they be sure? I mean I know one family and, out of three kids, two of them are gay. How do I know that when I'm thirty I'm not going to find out that I'm a lesbian like my mom did?" She is presently involved in all of the accepted social activities of heterosexual youth and speaks of her boyfriend with obvious enthusiasm, yet she does not trust her feelings to be permanent. She perceives her mother as having "changed" at the age of thirty-five, becoming something that she was not during her marriage. Her mother, Arlene, tells it differently.

"I always liked being with other girls and looking at them," she admits quietly. "But I had never heard of lesbians when I was growing up. I just assumed that I'd get married, have kids and forget about it. Well, I got married and had kids, all right, but I never quite forgot about it. And then, one day, I was watching the TV and I saw pictures from a gay freedom day celebration. Part of me was properly scandalized but part of me envied those people who dared to be different and follow their feelings. The women in the pictures looked so happy and alive. I couldn't get their faces out of my mind and, eventually, I realized that this was something I'd been hiding for twenty years. I didn't change, I just began expressing what I really felt deep down. My family had never had an inkling; it seemed like some Jekyll-and-Hyde change to them."

What most gay parents know, but may not have thoroughly explained to their children, is that the question of why some people are gay has never been satisfactorily answered. The classic profile of a domineering, possessive mother and an absent or weak father simply does not apply in the majority of cases. Experimentation with hormones, popular at one time, shed little light. Stress in the womb, childhood illnesses and social conditioning have all been held responsible for creating homosexuals, but none of them quite bears up under empirical study. By now, many gays have reached a point of saying, "Who knows why we're gay? We *are* and we have a right to be happy." This is a major step forward. For too many years gay men and lesbians accepted the verdict that they were "sick." Although many psychiatrists have claimed to be able to "cure" gayness, the success rate for changing a person's orientation is extremely low. Today, the psychiatric community recognizes that homosexuality does not, of itself, constitute a psychological aberration. It is the guilt and confusion brought on by social pressures to be straight that causes neurosis. Children whose parent is gay should realize that their parent is not sick but is simply a member of a significant minority group.

Homosexuals comprise somewhere between 4 and 13 percent of the total population of North America (depending on which study you accept) and it has been well documented that homosexuality existed in the earliest civilizations. In all those centuries, we have not yet been able to explain why a certain minority prefer their own sex. Heredity does not seem to be a major factor. In the first place, as many gays and lesbians point out humorously, the majority of homosexuals were born to heterosexual parents. In the second, the majority of gays do not have children. Thus, if homosexuality were passed directly from parent to child, the tendency would have died out centuries ago. If homosexuality is truly linked to some recessive genetic trait, we will have to wait until science has further unraveled the mysteries of DNA to discover how. In the meantime, it is virtually impossible to predict, at birth, which child will be straight and which will be gay.

Our survey did find that some homosexuals had homosexual children, but the overall number was well within the expected range of the population at large—somewhere around 7 percent. It would seem that the children of gays have about the same chance of being gay as the children of heterosexuals. Parental example set little precedent: there were gay sons of lesbian mothers, lesbian daughters of gay fathers, and heterosexual children, both of whose parents were gay. Ironically, while the children were worried mostly about heredity, courts and parents seem more concerned with the possible influence of the parental environment.

Children who fear that they will turn out gay simply because one or both of their parents was gay, should relax. The evidence is quite reassuring. As summarized by Martha Kirkpatrick, M.D., of

U.C.L.A.: "evaluation . . . revealed no indication of differences in gender development between children brought up by lesbian mothers and those raised by unmarried heterosexual mothers."

Yet the fear *does* need to be addressed so that the child can attain peace of mind and the assurance that her or his affectional preference is a matter of individual choice. Clear and informed communication between parent and child is the best means to achieve this. If communication has deteriorated or the anxiety persists despite efforts to reassure the child, by all means seek out professional counseling. A list of counseling services familiar with gay family issues is included in the resources section of this book (Appendix One). Your local gay services center or hotline may also be able to refer you to an experienced counselor. Talking to other children of gays can also be helpful. Some of these kids have had the same questions and fears. Their feedback is relevant and nonthreatening and may be much easier for a teenager to accept.

Lindsay, fifteen, participated in the children's auxiliary of a gay fathers' group for several years.

> When I was younger, I laid awake nights thinking, "God, I might be gay when I'm older." That's really scary—here my dad is, maybe it runs in the blood or something! I know that's not really true now; I know I'm straight.
>
> If a person finds out that a parent is gay when they're my age, they pretty much know whether they're straight or not. However if a child finds out their parent is gay, I think it's better for the parent to explain to them . . . just sit and talk with them and say, "Hey, this is the way it is with my life and you do not have to copy me. You're not supposed to copy your parent, you're supposed to grow as you want."
>
> . . . If you're a seven-year-old and you find out your dad or mother were gay, you just might question it more like, "Maybe I'll be like them," because when they're that age, they want to be like Mommy or Daddy, so I think it is good to talk to them when they're young.
>
> I think it's a lot better to tell the young child because then they don't have their own opinion. My age-level group, it's a lot of peer pressure—"Okay, you've got to be straight!" I'm sixteen and that's where sex starts coming into life—the relationships and everything. When they're younger, they don't have that peer pressure, so if they know then, it's a lot easier. However if they're older . . . and they find out that their

parent is gay, it's very hard for them because they've been brought up for so many years thinking everybody's supposed to be straight—so it's very hard for them to accept their parents. The young child will love Mommy and Daddy no matter what."

As lesbians and gay men, many of us have experienced the pain of social rejection to some extent. We may have examined sex roles and patriarchy and rejected them as limiting. We raise our children, hoping that they will be free of prejudice and narrow-minded attitudes. We want them to be secure, to be strong, to be free of stereotypes and sexism. And yet . . . and yet, who among us does not want our children to have friends? We hope that there are other parents with attitudes like our own, raising open-minded children. We hope that we have taught our kids to choose their friends wisely. Most of all, we hope that our sexual orientation does not adversely affect our children's social adjustment.

In some instances, concern over socially stigmatizing a child keeps parents in the closet or sends them running right back to it at the first sign of trouble. Elaborate ruses may be manufactured to explain to neighbors, friends, etc., who that other adult is in your household. How many gay and lesbian lovers have been introduced as "Sally's aunt Jean" or "Bob's uncle Charlie" in an attempt to plant the assumption that the lover is a relative of some sort? How many people maintain separate (and expensive) households in order to substantiate the deception?

It is the parents, primarily those who are not out in the community or are not comfortable with their sexuality, who are most concerned with this issue. Few, if any, of the children initiate deception. The younger kids simply aren't aware of the social ramifications; the older ones are sophisticated enough to remain quiet if they suspect a negative reaction from their peers. Indeed, one of the outstanding traits common to children of lesbians and gays is their caution. Lindsay again:

> The only people I ever really told were people that I felt could pretty much accept the fact . . . I never really told acquaintances or people I just knew from class, people who, when I said, "My Dad's gay," would say "Oh, you poor thing!" which is a lot of the reaction I got. I only told people that I trusted, that I pretty much knew.

Out here [Oklahoma] I have to make sure they're not going to tell anybody, that it's not going to go around town, because I'd be the laughingstock of the whole town; they'd point at me all up and down the street. Word travels quickly around here. Out there [New York City] I didn't really care if everybody knew because it was such a normal thing, but here I only tell people I really trust . . . only friends of mine. I would not want them to tell their parents. You have to realize that out here it's like "the Bible says . . ."—that's the way they are. I would be evil or something because I'd be part of a gay man, you know? So that's why I make sure it's closed. I say, "I told you, just put it in the back of your head, just don't talk in your sleep."

Why did you tell anyone?

Because I thought they needed to know, because they would ask . . . sometimes I'll mention something that sounds kind of funny, like when I say, "My dad and Bob . . ." I kind of have to explain that. I never mention my dad and Bob to anybody I don't really know; I'll say "My dad out in New York" . . . if I mention Bob, I make sure they understand why they live together. It's none of their business really, unless I want to tell them; they don't have any right to ask me, but if I decide to tell them, that's my business and theirs and just ours between us.

Is it still true that you haven't told any guys out here yet, just girls?

I had a boyfriend a couple of months ago and I didn't even tell him. That was because he was real straight and I knew that if I told him, it would hurt; he wasn't really a boyfriend; we were just having fun, just going out, and I didn't feel that it was any of his business so I didn't tell him.

When I tell somebody my dad's gay, even my good friends, I don't make sure that we have a quiet room and we sit down and really discuss this, I say, "Oh, yeah, my dad's gay," in a by-the-way sort of thing . . .

It never bothered my sexuality. It did kind of bother my social life a little bit; I didn't have friends come over a lot. I mean, I did have good friends over, but not like, "Hey, let's have a party at my house"—that kind of thing. I did have a couple of boyfriends out there and . . . when I thought they would understand, they didn't . . . But I figured, well, that's their problem, not mine. I did have one guy I was dating who came in. He was really interested in English and my father was an English major . . . they had about half an hour's conversation . . . I didn't have to say a thing . . . He seemed to like my father a lot . . . but then, I didn't like him, so . . .

. . . I wouldn't want to have been in the position I'm in now ten years ago . . . I don't think I'd be this open. I don't think I'd be doing this interview, but it's okay now.

People have called my dad a faggot when I've walked with him on the street and, oh, that galls me! I've had fantasies of actually going up to these guys . . . and telling them, "Never talk to my father that way!" The people who don't let themselves have an open mind—that's what makes me mad!"

This attitude of protectiveness is not uncommon. Even when the children themselves have mixed feelings about their parent's homosexuality, they can be staunch defenders if the parent comes under attack. Now eighteen, Richard has lived with his lesbian mother and her lover since the age of twelve.

"Sure, there are times when I wish we were just a normal family," he says, "But my mom and Liz are okay. If people can't handle it then . . . well . . . they're not the kind of people I want to know—bigots and stuff. If somebody was here and made a crack or something, I'd probably kick 'em out. People should be able to do what they want in their own houses. I don't have to do it myself to stick up for what's right!"

It would be reassuring to say that the children of gays are not affected socially by their parent's orientation, but it would not be truthful to do so. Once again, children under the age of ten appear to be fairly immune to social pressures of this sort.

In quite a few adolescents, however, there is a certain seriousness toward life and friendship that goes beyond the socialization typical of the average teen. They appear more cautious and analytical about relationships in general and seem to approach their close friendships with more conscious forethought. Some of them are more "adultified," taking responsibility and communication as sacred trusts. They have a "secret" that most choose to share with discretion, knowing that a misplaced comment to the wrong individual can have lasting repercussions. A few have become loners, more comfortable with their parent's adult friends or with books and study. More often, however, they seem to acquire a few close and trusted friends and remain loyal to those few who respect their secret. Only the boldest, most outgoing kids expressed an "I don't care who knows" attitude.

So there are effects, occasionally quite profound, for adolescent children of gay parents. The question then becomes, are these effects necessarily negative? And the answer is no, not in the long run. While many of the children curb their revelations out of concern of ostracism or harassment, only one of those I spoke with had experienced any criticism or direct homophobia. Whether this is a sign of the success of their circumspection or a reflection of indifference on the part of peers is impossible to know for sure. And, overall, the older children tended to speak of this caution as a positive thing, helping them to overcome personal prejudices, teaching them to be better judges of character and to choose friends for their intelligence and judgment rather than for external considerations. Says Llana Lloyd, founder of Children of Gays:

> My friendships as a child were stronger than most, because I picked my friends carefully. I chose them for what was inside, not on appearances; I knew that I could trust them to stick by me. And they did. In that respect, I think that I was fortunate. Having a lesbian mother made me stop and think of myself in relationship to other people. It made me open-minded and I chose friends who were open-minded and we learned a lot from each other that way.

Sexism and Gay and Lesbian Parenting

When asked during an interview if there was anything he felt should be included in a book for gay parents, Chris, a Midwestern doctor with two small boys, nodded his head emphatically.

"I'd like to see people reminded that it's not just gay issues we're involved with; it's broader than that. It's sex-role issues, male-female issues, patriarchal issues . . . lots of things. What we're up against—it's television commercials, it's cereal boxes, it's clothing. It's everywhere . . ."

It may seem redundant to address sexism in a gay-oriented book. Those of us who were aware of our gayness at an early age have lived through the anguish of trying to conform to society's expectations about our gender roles. The rigid codes of behavior set out for each sex evoked, in many of us, a sense of guilt, shame or failure as we struggled unsuccessfully to fulfill them. It is hoped that we have come to realize how unhealthy sexist expectations are and to reject sexist models of behavior. We have learned to transcend the conditioning that promotes sex-linked expectations. Or have we?

"The other morning my daughter, Shannon, was getting ready for school," said Jean, the lesbian mother of two. "She came out in an old sweatshirt and I heard myself saying, 'why don't you wear your white blouse, hon, it's so much prettier.' I mean, I really *heard* myself. I didn't say she should wear the blouse because it looked better or because the sweatshirt had holes, but because it was *prettier!* I'd never tell my *son* to wear something prettier, but I realized I do it to my daughter all the time. I think I'm so liberated—I was wearing jeans and a T-shirt myself at the time—but the conditioning to think in terms of girls and boys is insidious. I tell Danny to be practical and then send signals to Shannon telling her that it's more important to be pretty. That's part of the old double standard that screwed me up; I don't want my kids to get it dumped on them too. I watch myself more closely these days."

Jean's point is valid. If each of us had not rebelled against the behavior automatically expected of us by virtue of our sex, we would not be any less gay. We would be unhappy, frustrated people struggling against a locked closet door. Sexist expectations were not good for us; we cannot expect them to be any better for our children, whatever their affectional preference turns out to be.

Are you saying at this point, "I'm gay, I can't be sexist"? Consider then that more than 50 percent of the parents who were out to their kids said that they had (or would have) handled the revelation differently with their daughters than with their sons and that they tended to treat the boys and girls differently.

"Girls are more understanding, more open-minded than boys" was a statement I heard time and time again. Statistically, it appears to be true: daughters rarely expressed outright rejection of a gay parent while sons tended toward initial rejection followed by later acceptance. But assuming that girls have a natural propensity toward understanding is grossly unfair to the millions of open-minded boys in the world. And assuming that boys are less likely to be understanding is, to some extent, a self-fulfilling prophecy.

Some parents have promoted sexist standards because of their concern about custody cases. Many parents who had gone through a custody battle emerged very pleased that their daughters had been determined to be thoroughly "feminine," their sons genuinely "masculine" by contemporary standards. For the best of motives, they had fostered society's standards upon their children, even when those were the very standards that had worked to undermine their personal sense of self-esteem and integrity.

One lesbian mother admits to being very conscious of this process.

"When Jim was fighting me for custody of Tina," she says, "I knew that the judge would be looking at me in terms of what kind of daughter I was raising. So, during that period, I made sure that Tina wore dresses to school, had pink curtains in her bedroom and lots of 'girl toys.' You couldn't even see her bed it was so covered with dolls and stuffed animals. It worked: the social worker who visited wrote in her report that Tina had a very normal home environment—meaning, I guess, that she was being raised as a traditional girl." Her feeling was that the end result justified the means.

Generally, however, I found the daughters of lesbian mothers most likely to be receiving the encouragement and benefits of nonsexist attitudes. The sons of these same women presented a greater challenge: the mothers felt that social pressure toward "masculine" behavior in boys is more powerful than the pressure put on girls to be "feminine." According to Beth, an adoptive mother and lesbian activist:

"The issue of boy children in the lesbian community is one of the biggest issues, an issue of terribleness. A lot of lesbians are separatist; they want 'women only' space. They don't want to accept boy children over twelve years, yet a lot have precisely kids of that age and older. A lot of women have been ousted from [lesbian] collectives because their boy children grew older. It's an issue of not destroying the boy child's self-image because of how [these] women feel about men. There are boys becoming men who are just as obnoxious as men can be. What does a mother do, who's both a feminist and a lesbian, when she sees her son becoming a cultural male?"

There is no clear-cut answer yet to this question. While some women have made a conscious effort to educate their children along nonsexist lines, treating them as people regardless of sex, others have given up in despair, feeling overwhelmed by the thoroughness of the job that schools, television and older family members had already done to convince the youngsters that macho is superior. Those who practice a form of reverse sexism by discriminating against boys are apparently in the minority, yet their effect is felt strongly enough that a number of women surveyed made reference to the issue.

"The National Women's Music Festival will not allow male children over seven on the property," says Sondra, calling the situation "tragic." "There are many separatists in the lesbian community. While I guess I understand their position intellectually, I don't emotionally agree with that. The women that I know who have boys love their sons, and all of us who are their friends love their sons."

And Gretchen, who has lived with her son in a number of different locations, adds, "I've seen that some women feel that they need to politically condition their kids and it has turned me off . . . It can make it so complicated that it cramps the ability to raise children who are alive to the realities of day-to-day life. The boys being raised by lesbians seem to be more serious and oppressed, whereas the girls tend to be a bit freer and more enjoying of childhood."

Most of these women agree that the primary influence toward this reverse sexism is not the mothers themselves but nonparents who do not perceive that parenting is what Gretchen describes as "a love chore."

Gay fathers also treated sons very differently than daughters for the most part. Like their straight counterparts, many of them refrained from physical or emotional expressions of affection, passing on a long-lived legacy of "masculinity" dependent on emotional repression. These were the same men who had struggled to break away from conventional expectations and conditioning and come to terms with their gayness. On the other hand, many gay fathers were extremely close to their daughters, developing a rapport and understanding unusual between male parents and female children. They could open up to the girls, they felt, without compromising the child's gender orientation for, as the myth goes, girls are "naturally" more open and affectionate than boys.

Ron, the noncustodial father of four, put it thus:

"My daughters received more of the benefit of my coming out than my sons did. I felt I could be open with them, that they'd accept my being affectionate and emotional. I was more careful with the boys—afraid that they'd see that kind of behavior as 'sissy.' You know how teenagers are."

The minority of parents who genuinely practiced the philosophy of encouraging individual inclinations over gender-specific conditioning seemed to have good all-around relationships with children, male and female. From their own struggle against labels and social boxes, they had learned that developing the potential of the *person* their child is, rather than the child's assumed gender-specific traits, gives the child a sense of competence and worthiness. By allowing boys and girls to express their feelings and thoughts freely, without judging them as inappropriate, they encouraged creativity and self-reliance. As one teenage girl put it, "The best thing my dad gave me was the feeling that it was all right to be me and have my own ideas and opinions—and know that he'd stand behind me." What more precious gift can parents give to children than this sense of their own strength and self-worth?

FIVE

Lovers

When Fred's son first came to live with us, he was a terror and I wasn't sure that we could become family . . . Fred told me that he was a sweet, charming, cute little boy. He is—when he's sleeping—but he's also a little devil.

CARL, age thirty-five, lover of a gay father

"The kids are a part of my life," Adam commented during his interview, "It's a package deal that a boyfriend is getting. What you see is what you get—and I come with children . . . I wouldn't particularly like to date someone who was uncomfortable with my having kids; it would put a rift in there that would be difficult to work around."

The lesbian woman or gay man who chooses to become involved with a parent needs to be aware that, along with the adult relationship, she or he is also getting a relationship with that adult's offspring. This is particularly true if the parent has custody of minor children whose daily well-being he or she must look out for. Lovers will not be the sole object of affection or attention; they may well find themselves a second priority, however much loved. Instead of socializing with friends, spending quiet evenings alone together or keeping flexible schedules, the gay couple raising children have PTA meetings and school plays on their agenda.

Even noncustodial parents living miles away from their children present a unique challenge to their lovers. Unlike ex-lovers or spouses who may be virtually forgotten or despised and written off, children are a part of oneself in an intimate way that is difficult to refute or ignore. The bond between parents and children affects many aspects of both their lives, whether the relationship is good or bad.

Sylvia, a lesbian of forty, has been prevented from any contact with her three teenage daughters and presently lives in a city some 1,200 miles distant from them. Yet her motherhood is constantly with her. Reflecting upon the breakup of a recent relationship, she commented, "My lover didn't understand my feelings about the kids, she resented the time I spent talking about them. Sometimes I'd cry because I missed them so much and it would make her mad because I was unhappy and not fun to be around. She really minded that the kids had such an influence on me when they weren't there."

The attachment of parent and child can prove incomprehensible to a nonparent, just as the children themselves may seem alien and unmanageable. Some women and men open themselves gladly to the influence of a child, some are unable or unwilling to do so. In the latter case, the love relationships appear to have a short life expectancy.

Like Adam, many of the parents interviewed expressed strong doubts about their willingness to become involved with anyone awkward with or opposed to the children. "The kids come first," many of them say emphatically. "My other relationships have to be worked around that!" The would-be lover who walks in unprepared for that primary rule is in for a few surprises.

A significant number of those who responded to our survey indicated that they had observed some degree of jealousy or competition between their children and their lovers. The younger (under ten) children seemed most often to be jealous of their parents' affections while the lovers were reported to compete more with older children and teenagers. A few parents admitted that their own fears and guilt (both about being gay or lesbian and about splitting their affections) were the biggest factor contributing to tensions between their lover and their children. All in all, the adults had a much more difficult time accepting the children than the other way around.

"My lover couldn't understand that there are times that I have to be with my kids," was a frequent comment. "My friends and lovers don't realize that I don't have the disposable income that they, as single adults, have to spend," was another. For many gay men and lesbians, involvement with a parent brings the first exposure to children since their own childhood—and the exposure can be an eye-opener.

Yet for all the potential problems, it is interesting to note that more than half of the custodial gay fathers and two thirds of the custodial lesbian mothers reported that they were presently involved in a significant love relationship. Many of these were partnerships of long duration, as successful, by traditional standards, as any heterosexual marriage. Clearly then, being a parent doesn't preclude the opportunity to establish a strong gay or lesbian relationship. Indeed, many partners indicated that the presence of a child reinforced their commitment and enriched their lives.

Says Carl: "The strongest bond in our household is between Fred and I, but Steven [Fred's ten-year-old son] plays a very big part in that. If he weren't in our relationship . . . [it] wouldn't be as strong as it is . . . A thread becomes stronger the more that you intertwine it with other threads. Three strands wrapped together become that much tougher to break . . . instead of our thinking 'Could we possibly break up?' we're more apt to think 'When can we afford a house big enough for the three of us?' "

Even in the cases where relationships collapsed during the course of the survey, children were rarely stated to be the direct cause of the breakup. Indeed, some foundering affairs have been helped or prolonged by the influence of one partner's children.

Sometimes, a person's being a parent was a factor in the lover's initial attraction to them.

Sondra is a psychotherapist. An attractive woman of fifty, she recently ended a one-year relationship with June, age thirty-two.

"I'm sure that if she didn't have a child I wouldn't have considered becoming involved with a woman as young as she is. Not that she wasn't a charming, lovely woman; she was. Only I might have been a little more cautious because of the age difference. But I love children. Absolutely love children.

"I'm quite sure that June didn't get in touch with the reality that she wasn't in love with me earlier because she so much enjoyed my sharing the parenting of David, her son. I'm quite sure that I overlooked the fact . . . for a longer period of time because of David. It took me a long time to get out of my own head that both he and I would survive [the breakup]."

Some parents indicated that their lovers had better rapport with their kids than they did themselves. The degree of responsibility assumed by the parents' partners did not appear to have any bearing on this: few lovers were regarded as a "soft touch," attempting to win the children over by gifts or permissiveness. Rather, the children viewed these persons as sympathetic ears, people who cared, who had a stake in the family's life, but who had come into the situation without judgment of what had gone before. Much of this depended upon the nonparent's willingness to be integrated into the family environment, to become involved emotionally and intellectually with children as well as parents. According to Fred: "[My son] Steven looks at Carl as a second father figure." Carl agrees.

"I probably spend more time with Steven than his dad does. I'm here more often when he needs someone to talk to . . . because his dad works strange hours and longer hours than I do . . . If he can't get hold of his father, he'll call me at work."

Frequently both partners assumed equal shares of discipline, recognizing that the adults in any family are responsible for primary decisions. Excluding one of the pair from taking part in decision-making which affects the family tends to put that person in a secondary position and may create friction and resentment. A few individuals felt that less involvement between lovers and children was preferable to the slow process of integration; these were generally noncustodial parents or their partners, and there was corresponding lack of closeness between the children and the parents themselves. These parents had compartmentalized their relationships, allocating specific times for specific people, and they were uncomfortable with any overlap. A few lovers expressed regret that the parental partners' anxiety or closeted status kept them from establishing a nurturing relationship with the children.

One young man who spoke to us was deeply involved with a noncustodial parent. Coming from a large family, he has always enjoyed children and child-raising. His lover, Dan, has two teenage daughters who know nothing of their father's relationship with Joseph. He has been presented as a neighbor and friend, included in a few family outings, but has had little opportunity to develop a relationship with the two girls. Although he would like to become more involved in parenting, he respects his lover's choice to keep him uninvolved. Prior to his relationship with Dan, Joseph lived with another man and his three children. In that situation, Joseph shared the parenting responsibilities equally with his lover and immensely enjoyed the challenge of raising children. They were a part of each other's lives to the extent that Joseph took them to his own family's gatherings, in the manner of a stepparent. Although the relationship eventually disintegrated, he remains in contact with the kids, visiting occasionally and talking with them by phone. He has enjoyed the parenting role so much, he says, that he hopes some day to be able to adopt his own children.

A 1984 study of gay male couples (*The Male Couple,* by A. Mattison and D. McWhirter) indicates that it is rare for gay men to pool their financial resources as straight couples generally do. Therefore it is not surprising that very few of the women who responded to our survey and virtually none of the men shared financial responsibility for a lover's children, whether or not they lived in the same household. A few lesbian couples had joint accounts that handled the entire family's expenses, particularly if both of them had children. The one exception among the men was a noncustodial father whose child-support payments were made from a checking account to which he and his lover contributed equally.

More commonly, the parent's partner contributes such extras as gifts, carfare, entertainment costs and occasional clothing, expenses which are not regular. Additionally, many lovers provide childcare while a parent works or attends school, help with rides to various activities and assistance with reading stories or homework. More than a few children owe a higher grade point average to tutoring by their gay parents' lovers.

For a single parent, any extra income or free time can be a blessing. None of the parents or lovers with whom we corresponded gave any indication that the lovers' input was expected or demanded. Most of the parents were grateful for someone with whom to share both the responsibility and the good times; financial arrangements were very flexible and varied. Among those parents who were not currently involved with another adult, more than a few wished for a relationship—not to aid them with the rigors of parenthood, but to have another adult with whom to share the special moments.

Living arrangements seemed a major concern for many lesbian and gay parents. Whether custodial or not, the question of whether to live with a lover was often a dilemma. For those parents not yet out to their children and families, the idea of living with a lover increased the likelihood that someone would discover their orientation. It is not usual, in our society, for two adults of the same sex to share a bedroom, much less a double bed. It is difficult to conceal such an arrangement from visiting children; impossible to conceal if they live with you.

A few of the noncustodial parents took two-bedroom apartments, specifically to hide the fact that the "roommate" was really a lover. This ruse works fairly well when the children are infrequent scheduled visitors. If the kids come and go randomly or spend much overnight time, however, the musical-bedrooms game becomes awkward and frustrating. Once again resentment arises as the lover is sent to her or his room because the children are visiting. And young minds put subtle clues together with amazing accuracy. The forgotten bedroom slipper, the wrong brand of cigarettes on a bedside table—these things are noted.

To be sure, subterfuge is warranted in some situations. Where there is a custody dispute, for example, the lesbian who shares her bed with another woman may find that such togetherness is viewed dimly in court. Something as simple as separate bedrooms may be enough to cast reasonable doubt in a judge's mind about the mother's alleged "moral deficiency" should the lesbian issue be raised in court.

Gretchen, thirty, lives in the suburbs of a large Midwestern city with her ten-year-old son Erik and Katharine, her lover of three years.

I came out to my son because of my present relationship, which is my first with a woman. When Katharine moved in, I had to discuss with Erik that some things, like gays and our relationship, couldn't be discussed with his grandparents. It was an immediate thing that we had to deal with . . . . My son knew from the very beginning that there was a difference between what was going on at our house and what goes on anyplace else. . . . It was six or seven months after Katharine moved in that we sat down to talk it over with Erik. It was brought on because he mentioned something inadvertently to my father and my mother told me about it. I haven't discussed the sexual aspects of our relationship with my mother, but I do discuss the emotional part; she understands we aren't "roommates" and is supportive. She cares a great deal for Katharine. I'd say yes if she asked if we were gay, but I'm not going to invite that.

You know, I visualized myself as a parent long before I saw myself being with a long-term lover, but being a single parent didn't sink in on me until I brought Erik home from the hospital for the first time; it's an enormous responsibility! I've had relationships with people all through my son's life but I chose to keep that part of my life separate from being a parent because it took a lot of energy to be single, raising a kid.

I had noticed that women together were a lot more intense and it was a lot more work than men living together. I avoided spending a lot of time with gay women for that reason—not consciously but subconsciously. It was just too much emotion, too demanding. I'm a Gemini, already too much into theatrics as it is. Before I met Katharine, I had felt that I was ready for a relationship, but I had been out of circulation and was busy as a parent so I wasn't sure how to make that happen. Before I met her, I had had two physical encounters with women, both uncomfortable; the idea was more attractive than the act. But it happened so naturally with Katharine, was so fulfilling, that I surprised myself. We spoke often at first about our surprise that we were both women; we didn't feel "gay" (whatever it's supposed to feel like), we felt we were just the right two women for each other.

Being a parent made it hard the first few months we were together; the excitement and experience of falling in love made me feel guilty. First, we were in a very small house; the desire to be physically intimate made me say, "Why is Erik here right now, why do we always have to wait for him to be asleep?" There wasn't ever enough time. At the same time as I felt guilty, I felt I really needed and deserved to go ahead and experience this. I felt so renewed. I was very anxious about Erik and Katharine, but I refused to make it an issue—their relationship, that is. Katharine was feeling the same way and making efforts to be with Erik when I could see that she was just interested to be with me. At the same time, Erik was becoming incredibly jealous, because for the first time in his life there was someone else who was more important than him a majority of the time. He withdrew a bit, then he pushed himself in the middle of us all the time, finding reasons to interrupt us. He felt left out. It didn't matter whether he was getting a positive or negative reaction from me; he wanted my attention and, after five or six months of this, I was questioning whether I had the energy to have a lover *and* be a parent. I talked about it with Katharine, but not too often because I didn't want to make it into a bigger thing than it was. It took the next six months after that to be able to acknowledge the times when it was getting in the way of our natural process of getting used to each other and settling down, to see the reality of it: we know we love each other, but can we live together? We had yet to establish a routine.

I went out a lot more that first year than I had for years: Katharine is younger, still active, in a career. There were a lot of compromises that I had to make. I'd be at work all day, then home as a mother, then to bed so I could get up early in the morning when Katharine came home so we could have some hours to ourselves. I became the real pulling force in the family; two people were looking for the attention they were used to getting. There weren't enough hours in the day to keep everyone happy. Once the romance period phased into family time and I went back to spending more time with Erik, he relaxed and Katharine got anxious. It reversed. I didn't really want to go out three nights a week and socialize. I'm basically somebody who likes home and others coming to visit. I told Katharine that I needed to start settling down somewhat. That's the hardest thing for a lover—to come into a relationship where there's a child. She needed to accept that there was another person in my life. I understood from the beginning that I couldn't expect her to love my son just because she loved me; it was a slower process and painful at times. Part of me said that the reason I am who I am is because I have a child; another part said, "Why should she have to love him, he's a different person than I am." I couldn't just go out when Katharine wanted to; I had to find a babysitter. In the morning I'd have to get Erik ready for school no matter what else was happening. I ended up taking it all on myself and thinking that I had to be a superwoman. After a while, I stopped doing that.

Katharine and I are pretty strict, though I'm a more passive parent than she is. She's very active in disciplining about school and his basic manners. I'm passive in that I can let him get real rowdy for a long time before I get down on him. I get real active toward his emotional maturity and I'm strict about his keeping up with household responsibilities. He's not living alone; I don't live alone and because we live with other people, certain things are demanded that might not be if we lived alone. You have to compromise and learn to pick up things even if you didn't put them there. We can negotiate how work gets done, but the fact that it has to be done is not negotiable. He shares the house and so he has a list of household things to do. This is important because I don't think that male or female roles can be defined according to what job you do. Erik also knows he has the freedom to enjoy the house.

Katharine and I don't disagree in front of Erik about authority or discipline areas; either we talk about them when he's not around or we decide together with him. We don't give him vast choices; it's usually "either this or this," two choices. I learned to let Katharine be an active 100 percent important person in decision-making in this household. There came a time when I gave myself to her enough that I realized I gave her my son too. Whether or not she wanted him was not the issue by that point; it was that I was committing not only myself but also committing Erik, because he's an integral part of me. We had to understand from the start that he's a permanent fixture in my world; he's not anything temporary. But being a parent is something that Katharine had to learn; she's not a natural parent, she doesn't consider Erik her "own," but she *does* consider herself a parent.

I'd like to see Erik and Katharine become closer friends; their relationship is taking a while, but it's an important process that we work on and encourage. Katharine's basic ideas about what's sane, moral, et cetera, are the same as mine and that makes it possible for me to look twenty or thirty years ahead to our being together. The importance of family, of home, of earning a living, are basics we were raised with and that we feel similarly about.

Overall, the keynote in integrating a lover into a gay or lesbian family seems to be patience. Each party involved must allow time for children and lover to grow accustomed to one another; then, perhaps, genuine affection may follow. Yet it cannot be expected in every case. Just as parents are not handed a warranty for parts and performance at the birth of their children, they are no more given a guarantee that the children will love (or even like) everyone the parents choose to love. They can hope that the children will respect their choice of partner and accept the parents' happiness as beneficial to the family.

The lover of a gay or lesbian parent must recognize the important role a child plays in his or her partner's life. Attempts to deny or negate that importance only serve to disrupt the love relationship, leading to resentment, misunderstandings and eventual breakup. Accepting the child as a separate individual with a personality quite distinct from that of the parent is also important, enabling lover and child to establish a relationship of their own. The ability to share another person's time and attention is a must, for both lover and child. Exclusivity is an unrealistic expectation: a caring parent spends time and energy on a child and consequently less time with a partner. Lovers can choose to share and participate in the enriching experience of parenthood, to remain detached and accept the ostensibly lesser input, or to fight against the parental attachment with the kids, a move that will most probably weaken the love relationship. They cannot expect, however, that the relationship will be unaffected by parenthood. The bond between parent and child is unique. The prudent lover honors this bond, the wise parent makes it clear from the onset of the relationship what priorities parenting imposes.

For many lovers of gay and lesbian parents, the relationship provides not only a challenge but a uniquely enriching experience: the opportunity to watch a child grow, to participate in the magic and excitement of childhood.

"I am so fortunate to have Scotty around," said one man, now in the sixth year of his relationship with a parent.

Having a ten-year-old around keeps me on my toes, keeps my feet on the ground. I learn something new at least once a week, just from being with him, talking with him. I think that there's a lot that gay people can learn about relationships and sharing from kids. It's so easy in the gay community to lose touch with the sense of continuity that a family, whether it's gay or straight, can provide. Children are really practical, their needs and experiences pretty straightforward; they haven't learned yet to play mind games. I know I've learned a lot about responsibility and saying what I really mean during these last six years.

SIX

Married and Gay

It will come as no surprise that more than 80 percent of the parents I talked to indicated that they had been married when their children were born. After all, for many years, the stigma against unwed mother(or father)hood was tremendous. Few mothers kept the babies conceived outside of marriage and single people were rarely allowed to adopt. Only recently has single, unwed parenthood by choice become an acceptable (though still radical) alternative to the nuclear family. My assumption from the start was that most gay and lesbian parents had married at one time, come out, divorced and were now raising their children as single individuals or with a lover.

Gay and lesbian parents' groups supported the assumption; often they are formed to offer legal aid and advice on custody issues and emotional support during divorce.

What *is* surprising is that 20 percent of the parents I contacted were still married and intend to remain so. The 20 percent excludes people who are separated or widowed but includes those who are married to gays of the opposite sex, for coparenting or convenience. Some of the most open and willing participants in interview situations were members, not of gay parents' groups, but of groups designed primarily to support married homosexuals.

Eighty-five percent of the still-married homosexuals were men. Only five lesbians indicated that they were currently married; four of these are coparents who chose to marry the gay fathers of their children-by-choice and one is still very much in the closet. Although there are a great number of support groups for gay married men, there do not appear to be any at all for their female counterparts. Conventionally married lesbians who are out to their spouses and children are scarce, at least we couldn't locate any. It seems that married lesbians who come out get divorced.

In contrast, many of the men were not only married but involved in second or third marriages. Most of them were out to their families and, not infrequently, engaged in long-term relationships with other men with their wives' knowledge and consent. In a few instances, correspondents said that their wives had been their staunchest, most supportive allies during the coming out process.

"I discussed my attraction for men with Marge before we got married," says Jeff, referring to his wife of eleven years. "I wanted everything to be open between us. Both of us were pretty naïve then. I thought it was a phase I'd pass out of if she'd be patient about it. She was pretty patient and understanding considering the circumstances, but I didn't grow out of it; it kept getting stronger. It tore me apart until I finally faced up to being gay. Telling Marge was the hardest part."

"I just kept thinking, 'This can't be happening to me,' " Marge, a pretty, soft-spoken woman, says, smiling. "I knew he'd had those feelings before, but I assumed that, after we'd been married, they'd sort of fade away. For a long time, I refused to accept it. Then I got mad; I cried a whole lot and said some pretty hateful things. That was a hard year."

Jeff nods. "We were like two strangers—always sniping at each other. We were ready to file for divorce, even though that meant telling the kids what was going on (Jason and Peggy are seven and nine respectively.)"

"Then, one day I looked at Jeff and said, 'Why am I so mad?' " Marge picks up the tale. "It wasn't like he hadn't warned me from the start. I realized that it was a thing about pride—like I wasn't enough of a woman to make him happy or something. I carried that around for a while and then finally confronted him with it. He convinced me that it wasn't me that was lacking—that he loved me and I satisfied him as much as he thought any woman could, but . . ."

"But that there was something in me that needed a man too," Jeff finishes. "Not instead—I felt clear on that. I didn't want to stop what we had had together. I mean, Marge and I were best friends. We were lovers too, but most important, she's my best friend and my kids' mother. That's a lot to lose. We talked about it for a long time and decided to try and stick with the marriage. That was four years ago. It's working out okay." He glances at Marge for confirmation and she nods decisively.

"Once we got over the initial shock, I found out that Jeff's being gay really didn't change that much in our lives. Honestly, he's happier now, more at peace, and so really it's made some improvements all around. It was hard at first thinking about sharing him with somebody else, but that was my upbringing more than my experience. As long as he doesn't take away from me and the kids to give to someone else, I'm satisfied. And he's happy. And the kids are normal, happy kids. They don't know about our . . . arrangement."

Their "arrangement" is that Jeff is free to go out and meet men as long as it doesn't interfere with the smooth flow of family life. For the first three years, he treated his night out as though he were going to a bowling league or night class—leaving the house after dinner on Fridays and returning sometime around midnight, never discussing his activities. In the last year, however, that has begun to change.

When he began to see one man, George, on a regular basis, he began to test the flexibility of his arrangement with Marge. At first it was different nights of the week rather than exclusively Fridays. Then an extra evening now and again. He was worried that this level of involvement would be perceived by Marge as a threat. Instead, she surprised him one day, suggesting that he invite George to spend time at their house on the evenings she had classes and Jeff stayed home to watch the children. Despite nervousness on everyone's part (particularly George's), the arrangement has worked so well that George is now a frequent visitor. He has dinner with the family at least one night per week, babysits occasionally and is called "uncle" by the two children. He shares Marge's keen interest in classical music and the two have become good friends, exchanging albums and even attending concerts together. "I haven't lost a husband," Marge chuckles during a private conversation, "I gained a cultural ally and a new friend. It may seem like a weird relationship, but—and I think this is because we were always honest with one another—it's actually worked out to everyone's advantage. Even the kids like it."

Although some people may find it weird, Jeff and Marge's story is not that uncommon. Most of the still-married gays I spoke to gave versions of the same basic events: a confession of homosexual attraction before the marriage, assumptions that they would pass, realization that they did not, coming out followed by anger, hurt, confusion and, in the end, acceptance of the situation and a conscious effort to sustain the marriage with as few waves as possible.

The characteristics of the individuals involved in successful "mixed" marriages were fairly consistent: a certain naïveté about homosexuality prior to the marriage, a history of honesty and communication, flexibility, a strong desire for the perceived benefits of marriage and a shared value system. Additionally, many of the women indicated that sex was not, nor had it ever been, a high priority in the relationship. Not that gay-straight marriages are sexless. In fact, most couples indicated that the frequency of their sexual activity had not significantly altered since the one partner's coming out. That frequency does not appear to be high, however: most such couples reported that sexual activity in their marriage had occurred from one to six times per month, placing them on the low end of the spectrum.

While the men, obviously, sought some sexual gratification outside of their marriage, the wives rarely, if ever, did. Most of them expressed no interest in extramarital relationships, saying that they were satisfied with what they had. A few had considered the option but never actively pursued it and a third handful voiced the traditional double standard that a man has greater need of sexual gratification than a woman and that it was okay for their mates to have other partners but not themselves. By and large, however, the majority of women married to gay men seemed disinclined to pursue extramarital sex for themselves, primarily because they do not perceive a need to do so. The success of their marriage was felt to be based on security, friendship and shared concern for their children, with sexuality tending to run a distant fourth.

Not everyone can successfully combine coming out and exploring homosexuality within a socially sanctioned heterosexual marriage. Despite the noteworthy percentage of men surveyed who were still participating in that institution, the fact remains that the majority of men and women who come out after marriage eventually divorce. It takes a truly remarkable bond with the spouse or a great ability to suppress the evidence of one's orientation to make these mixed marriages work. Often it is the spouse who is called upon to make a major adjustment based on a set of emotions and needs that are not her own and that came as a total surprise. She (remember that most married homosexuals are men) must be determined, open-minded and flexible if she is not to have her needs and priorities overwhelmed by the changes happening around her. There are people with such strengths out there and they are apparently making marriage work.

Counseling by educated professionals, support groups for spouses and monthly newsletters provide support for families in transition and in exploration. I spoke with families where one partner had been gay for many years. They had weathered the initial shock and storms, the guilts and jealousies, and found that their union was worth it all. Where the precedent of communication was established early on in marriage, the potential for remaining married regardless of primary sexual orientation seems good. Where family expectations and social conventions were the motivation for marriage in the first place, the bond was insufficient to maintain even friendship between many couples. Ultimately, whatever the circumstances surrounding the coming-out process, a decision was reached to stick it out and grow as a family unit or to break up the marriage and go separate ways. In the end, the more informed and communicative the partners, the happier and more amicable the final decision seemed to be.

So there are happily married homosexuals and they are more numerous than we might think. Those that choose to face issues of sexuality straight on are learning to make relationships work as gays, as partners and as friends. They too are champions of the right to choice.

SEVEN

The Impact of AIDS

"My kids worry about me," says Jeremy, a California father of two teenagers. "They worry about whether I'm happy, whether I'm going to end up alone. They worry a lot about me getting sick." He frowns a little. "They can handle my being gay just fine in theory but this whole AIDS epidemic has them scared. To tell you the truth, it's got me a little scared too."

The issue of health is a sensitive one for many gay fathers. In the last decade, the incidence of sexually transmissible diseases has reached epidemic proportions in the gay male communities of most major cities. With half of the patients at some city venereal-disease treatment centers citing homosexual contacts, with gay men listed along with health-care workers and intravenous drug users as high-risk groups for hepatitis B and now, with male homosexuals accounting for over two thirds of the victims of the potentially deadly acquired immune deficiency syndrome, there is reason to be concerned.

Venereal disease has always been a fact of life in the gay (male) community, but the practical attitude for a great many men was, "Sure it's awkward and unpleasant, but it's a risk you take. After all, this is the twentieth century. You go and get a shot. It's not like you're gonna die from it after all." Even the more serious hepatitis virus is rarely lethal in our modern world; painful, certainly, debilitating, yes; but almost no one dies from it anymore. So, to a lot of people, sexually transmissible disease was looked at as an acceptable and treatable risk, more an inconvenience than a real threat. Then, in 1981, acquired immune deficiency syndrome, commonly referred to as AIDS, rocked the gay communities of New York, California, Florida and other major cities across the country. From the onset it was quite obvious that a majority of the AIDS victims were gay or bisexual men.

Briefly, AIDS is a condition in which the body's natural immune system malfunctions, leaving it vulnerable to a variety of opportunistic infections and some previously rare forms of cancer. Because several manifestations are commonly present, AIDS is considered a "syndrome." The depressed immune response renders the body susceptible to infections that the healthy individual rarely succumbs to, such as Kaposi's sarcoma (a cancer) and pneumocystis carinii pneumonia, both of which are potentially fatal. For the AIDS patient with an already weakened immune system, even a simple cold can be deadly. No wonder then, that the word of a rising epidemic created a near-panic situation, not only among gay men themselves but in the population at large. Initial statistics showed that 95 percent of the victims were male. They fell into several high-risk categories: intravenous drug users, hemophiliacs who receive transfusions of blood and blood products, Haitian immigrants (though there is controversy over this) and male homosexuals. No one was more unhappy to learn this than the gay men who made up the largest single risk group (over 65 percent of male victims). As one man sadly put it, "It seems like we're coming out of the closet and into the morgue."

Initially, one of the biggest problems with AIDS was that no one knew what caused it or how it was transmitted. Given that two of the high-risk groups were defined specifically by their contact with blood (IV drug users and hemophiliacs) and that many of the gay men had engaged in oral or anal intercourse with the possibility of transmission through blood or semen (sperm-containing semen has certain characteristics in common with blood that make it possible for some viruses such as hepatitis B to be transmitted during intercourse), the initial supposition was that the infecting agent was carried in the bloodstream and directly transmitted (this as opposed to the possibility of airborne germs or virus). Scientists are now quite sure that AIDS is caused by a virus called HTLV-III. The initial panic generated by fear that AIDS could be casually acquired (by a handshake or circulating money, etc.) would appear to be unwarranted. The connection now seems to be intimate contact (intercourse, sharing needles, transfusions). Current studies show that in the absence of intimate contact, health-care workers taking care of AIDS patients, who would presumably be at the greatest risk if AIDS were an airborne disease, have no higher incidence of infection than the population at large.

Within the gay community, the AIDS epidemic has caused some splintering. Some people feel that the reaction has been disproportionate and that a great deal of harm has been done to gay liberation by a panicked populace. Others have retreated from their fellows, loudly denouncing most forms of sexual intimacy as self-destructive. And far too many have played ostrich, ignoring the signs and going along as though nothing much had changed. Politically, almost any stand one can take on AIDS prevention is dynamite; every position has its vehement foes.

For the gay father, AIDS has presented an additional complication. Because little is certain with regard to transmittal of the disease and because there is as yet no cure for this often fatal condition, the gay fathers we talked to felt particularly strongly about prevention.

"If I were the only one at risk, it wouldn't be so bad," one man said in an interview. "VD is one thing but with AIDS, well, it's the difference between playing hot potato and Russian roulette. I won't play Russian roulette with my kids' security; I don't have that option. So I have to be doubly careful who I sleep with and how. My kids need me—alive. And I don't know enough yet to be sure that they're not at risk of catching something if I do. I'm not taking any chances."

Transmission of AIDS is a subject of some fierce debate in both the medical and the gay communities. When the epidemic first became public knowledge, there was a tremendous reaction of fear, bordering on hysteria. Because researchers were unsure exactly what caused AIDS, they could only guess at how it was passed from one person to another (or even if it was a transmissible disease rather than a breakdown of the immune system due to overload). The fear of infection was fed by ignorance and homophobia. Hospital workers balked at treating AIDS patients, who were also frequently shunned by friends and family alike. One bus driver whose route passed through San Francisco's gay district adamantly refused to touch transfers that had been handled by passengers.

The often fatal nature of the disease has been so well publicized that even young children are aware of it. One young woman who counts a number of gay men as close friends recounts her experience taking her young niece to the first day of public school. As the school principal was taking them to the classroom, he commented casually, "You're lucky to be in Mrs. B.'s class: she has aides." The youngster froze in her tracks and stared at him.

"AIDS?" she asked, horrified, "Oh, no, I don't want AIDS! That's a disease; how can she have AIDS?" It took a while to reassure her that the principal had been referring to teaching assistants, not a disease. The story, while humorous, points up both the fear and awareness that have permeated our society.

At the time of this writing, advances are being made in the body of knowledge available regarding AIDS diagnosis and treatment. Despite inadequate research funding and public cooperation, work is under way to find a definitive diagnostic test as well as a cure and a vaccine. In the process, more information has evolved regarding the means of transmission of AIDS.

Contaminated blood or blood-containing matter appears to be the most likely means of transmission. The high-risk groups each come into contact with blood matter in some way—through contaminated syringes in the case of intravenous drug users, contaminated blood products in the case of hemophiliacs. Many of those outside the high-risk groups have received transfusions of potentially contaminated blood and most blood banks are currently refusing gay donors. In the case of the homosexual men who make up nearly two thirds of the known AIDS victims, the evidence supports a conclusion that anal intercourse is a major (though not exclusive) means of transmission. Whether this is due to contamination by blood in the feces or cracks in the skin and mucous membranes, or whether the virus is transmitted in semen, is not yet known. The "safe sex" precautions that are touted to protect against AIDS advise not taking any chances and avoiding any exchange of bodily fluids until there is a clear answer. It does appear pretty certain, however, that AIDS is not transmitted through casual contact; some exchange of body fluids, predominantly blood, appears to be necessary. Handling a bus transfer, therefore, will probably not give you AIDS unless someone has bled, defecated or ejaculated upon the transfer and you ingest or insert it into your own body.

"Intimate" (as opposed to "casual") contact is frequently interpreted as sexual contact. In terms of a transmissible disease, however, "intimate" can be construed as having physical contact with the body of another person to the extent that fluids or tissues may be touched and/or absorbed. This can take place during medical examination, accidents, etc., and is partly responsible for the nervousness of some health-care professionals regarding AIDS. Like any other transmissible disease, precautions are routinely taken and these precautions seem to work as well in preventing contamination by AIDS as they do in other diseases, or better.

What about the children? Are they at risk? This is a question being asked by thousands of gay fathers in metropolitan areas where AIDS is a known danger. Many of the men I talked to were concerned not only for themselves but for their children. "Am I running a risk of exposing my kids to something deadly by being a homosexual?" one man asked. Intimate contact in the form of diaper-changing, first aid, shared food, etc., is normal between parents and children, particularly very young children. Is this the type of contact that transmits the deadly virus?

The answers aren't all in yet; it may be years before those questions can be answered accurately. At this point we can only extrapolate from what has happened thus far and make judgments accordingly.

A few young children have contracted AIDS, but these children have all received contaminated blood transfusions or been born to mothers who were IV drug users or had had sexual contact with infected males. I could not find one instance among the several thousand diagnosed cases in which a child has acquired AIDS directly from an infected adult other than the mother (in utero). Yet there are gay fathers with AIDS, and as the epidemic runs its course their numbers are bound to increase. Concerns about the risk of their children being exposed to the disease need to be faced for the security of both parents and children.

If current research is any indicator, the type of contact required for transmitting AIDS is not customarily seen between parent and child. The one exception that I can think of would be blood or organ donations. It is strongly suggested that gay or bisexual men who need to make such donations be thoroughly screened. Although there is a test available for exposure to the infective agent (a retrovirus called HTLV-III) it is still not definitive: no one knows for sure exactly what the results of the test mean. Nonetheless, it is now being used by blood banks across the country to screen donated blood and efforts are being made to improve the test's overall accuracy. Of course, if you show any unusual symptoms or have had sexual contact with someone who now has AIDS, do not consider donating until more thorough screening and testing procedures have been developed.

As an additional caution, several gay legal and physicians' groups are advising that you only take the HTLV-III test under the supervision of a doctor whom you trust to protect your privacy and identity. While doctor-patient information is protected by law, there is some question about this confidentiality's extending to laboratories and blood banks. The concern is that your name and test results might end up on a list of those suspected of carrying AIDS. By labeling your blood sample with a code known only to your (trustworthy) doctor, rather than your name, this possibility can be reduced.

The other main concern regarding parenting and the transmission of AIDS arises when openly gay men contemplate biological parenting or sperm donation. If, as it appears, AIDS may be transmitted in sperm long before any symptoms appear in the victim, and if it is transmissible to a child in utero, a potential danger exists to all parties involved in the biological parenting process.

At a recent lesbian and gay parenting conference, the majority of women present stated emphatically that they would no longer consider using donor sperm from gay men. The men, likewise, expressed very real concern about the possibility of passing along the deadly virus to a child. At a time when more gay men and lesbians are contemplating parenthood, the AIDS epidemic strikes to the heart. Mothers of children conceived by unknown donor sperm and coparents whose child has a known gay father are now looking at their children with trepidation, wondering if the virus lies latent in them. And they wonder if they themselves might have the disease.

So far, none of the several dozen lesbians I talked to whose children were conceived with gay-donor sperm has had any indication that AIDS is a problem. But several dozen is hardly a statistic upon which to base predictions. When two children with bisexual fathers have come down with this disease, the potential seems clear. Symptoms have appeared by the age of eighteen months in children infected in utero—an incubation time shorter than that of many adults. This doesn't mean that children under eighteen months are in greater danger or that older children won't show signs; it is simply a guidepost for future understanding of the disease process.

So what can be done to prevent the possible in utero transmission of AIDS to the unborn children of gay men? How can the lesbian coparent or the gay donor feel safe about the conception process?

The answer is primarily the same as the one for men who ask, "How can I avoid contracting AIDS myself?" First and foremost, limit your activity to the "safe sex" practices that most gay health services recommend. These primarily involve eliminating the exchange of bodily fluids during foreplay and intercourse. For a more detailed description of "safe" sex practices, contact a local gay health agency or the AIDS hot lines listed in the resource section of this book. The second preventative measure for future parents is one that many people at the conference found difficult: time. Even if you currently practice safe sex, it does not mean that you have not already been exposed to the virus. The exception would be someone who has engaged solely in safe sex or has a relationship in which both partners have been 100 percent monogamous—for the past five years. One "unsafe" experience or one partner's infidelity negates the certainty of the parents' freedom from exposure to AIDS (though certainly the risk is substantially less than for those who commonly engage in unsafe sex with multiple partners).

Five years is the recommendation of the Bay Area Physicians for Human Rights, a group of concerned medical professionals who have made AIDS education a priority. Some doctors say three is sufficient because, at this time, three years is the longest known incubation period between exposure and the diagnosis of symptoms. BAPHR suggests five because, if three years is known, longer incubations may not have shown up yet. After all, AIDS has only been around a short time. Those concerned about the time element and what constitutes safe sex should contact an organization that can provide specific and up-to-date information about the latest findings.

Health screening at the present time will help eliminate a certain number of high-risk donors. But there is no definitive test for AIDS yet, and until it is available, extensive testing is of limited value in precluding AIDS. When it does become readily available, it will simplify the entire dilemma—for parents and nonparents alike.

So, in the face of this increasing health crisis, precautions should certainly be taken to safeguard ourselves and our children. Gay fathers and would-be fathers should monitor their sexual activity. A combination of safe sex and patience is urged for those who wish to procreate. Those who are currently safe but not ready to become fathers may consider having their sperm frozen at one of the several sperm banks willing to accommodate, so that future exposure to disease will not prevent parenthood. Lesbians in areas where AIDS is an issue are urged to avoid unknown gay donors whose sexual contacts might be questionable and to consider carefully any known donor or potential coparent whose history suggests a significantly increased risk of exposure. Blood or organ donations by gay fathers should be carefully monitored. Above all each of us needs to keep abreast of the latest developments regarding the epidemic.

The AIDS problem in the gay community does not present an impenetrable barrier against safe parenting; it does challenge us to be responsible and clearheaded when making our choices and decisions. The word is caution, not defeat. Bearing and nurturing children almost invariably presents us with personal limitations. If, in considering children, we balk at health safety measures because we find them limiting, it may be that we should rethink our priorities and our commitment to parenting.

EIGHT

Coparenting

Creating Alternative Families

Ellen and Todd live in San Francisco. She has a modern apartment near her downtown advertising agency. He shares a spacious flat with two other men. Their daughter Jamie Lynn spends three days a week with each of them; Sundays are shared—trips to the zoo, family dinners, outings in the park. Jamie's nursery school was chosen for its location midway between their separate homes. This sounds like a typical joint-custody arrangement—except that both Ellen and Todd are gay, they have never been married and Jamie Lynn was conceived through artificial insemination. Ellen and Todd are "coparents"—a growing phenomenon in the gay community today.

Webster's Collegiate Dictionary defines the prefix "co" as: ". . . importing rights or liabilities which are joint or in common

. . . with the sense of 'in or to the same degree.' " A "coparent" chooses to assume an equal portion of all parenting duties—physical, emotional and financial.

At first glance the word may seem redundant. Aren't all parents, straight, gay or lesbian, essentially "coparents," equally responsible for their offspring? A court of law would say yes, both parties involved in bringing a child into this world share an equal obligation to provide for that child. And yet one need not be a behavioral psychologist to see that it is the rare child whose parents each take on 50 percent of the upbringing, or enter into parenting with roles clearly thought out and defined, sometimes to the point of legal contracts.

The word "coparent" evolved as such clearly delineated parental relationships began to emerge. First and foremost, to be a coparent is to be a *parent by choice,* entering into the parenting process with forethought and a desire to assume a position of importance in a child's life *in tandem with one or more other responsible adults.* Coparents share responsibility for rearing a child, with the emphasis on the offspring rather than the relationship between the adults involved. This distinguishes coparenting from single parenting and from conventional marriage. A unique approach to child-rearing, it appears to be on the increase, particularly in the gay and lesbian community, where the demands of single parenting are not particularly welcome and conventional (i.e., heterosexual) marriages are out of the question (although it is not at all unusual for the gay and lesbian coparents to opt for marriage for a variety of practical and financial reasons). Coparenting, whether between gay men and lesbians or through various means between same-sex partnerships, is a viable alternative, offering a sharing of responsibility without the limitations of conventionality.

At a recent forum sponsored by the Gay Men's Parenting Group of San Francisco, a panel of six people, all coparents, fielded questions from a standing-room-only crowd. Both the panelists and the questions covered a wide range of topics related to this new phenomenon. By far the question that seemed foremost on everyone's mind was: how do you find someone to coparent with?

If any one method stood out from the others, it was friendship. Of the four different partnerships represented by the panelists, only one began as a pairing of strangers, both interested in parenthood and coming together for that purpose. All the others had begun as friendships, with a mutual desire for children leading the friendship into a coparenting agreement. This trait of friendship seems to hold true for other coparents across the country, particularly when the arrangement occurs between opposite-sex partners. Among the same-sex coparents, the desire for children more often evolved out of the partners' love relationship. Many of these were lovers of long duration, couples who had established a secure and stable home and wished to expand their union into a family.

Newspaper personal columns have received a great deal of attention lately as a method of reaching out to compatible partners. Along with word-of-mouth notices, personals were suggested in the forum as one potential way of finding a coparent. The advantage of wide circulation is undeniable; the drawbacks include possible crank responses, and all the obvious problems and awkwardness of screening responses and discussing such as personal a matter as conception with strangers. The screening process for a coparent would have to be even more extensive than that for a sperm donor (as discussed in Chapter Nine). Not only is the individual's genetic history and physical appearance up for scrutiny; past history and personality play a much more important role. And also unlike artificial insemination by donor (AID), both (or all) parties contemplating the step will be screening for fitness, with the potential mother's background and genetics as important to the would-be partner as the donor's qualifications are to the AID mother.

No wonder then that the majority of coparents began as friends. Friends with a common goal—to have and raise children. Friendship implies compatibility, common interests, mutual acquaintances. Friends often know one another's families, lessening the risk of awkwardness there. They know each other's habits, good and bad. How consistent and responsible is the potential coparent? A long-term acquaintance knows that, knows the partner's capacity to express thoughts and feelings. Communication, that most essential quality in any relationship, has already been established.

When Gwen, thirty-eight, moved from Tucson to Quebec to live with her lover Marie, it was understood that they would investigate the possibility of raising a baby together. It soon became obvious, however, that Marie was not prepared to be a parent.

"She was too set in her ways," Gwen recalls. "And clean! I mean, I'm no slob but this woman would wear the same white suit to work all week and, on Friday, it would look like it just came back from the cleaners! My cat drove her crazy. I spent half the relationship running around defuzzing the upholstery. It finally dawned on me that if she couldn't handle one reasonably tidy woman and a cat, she'd never deal with dirty diapers and spilled cereal."

While they were trying to work things out, Gwen renewed her friendship with Claude, a gay man ten years her junior. Recognizing the prolonged red tape of immigration, they married, sealing a bond which has endured. Claude was close to his own family, compassionate and good with kids. He wanted children of his own one day. He was, Gwen realized, excellent father material—intelligent, healthy and attractive. Shortly after her relationship with Marie ended, Gwen and Claude moved back to Tucson and conceived their daughter, Natalie. They describe themselves as "coparents and partners. Most of all, we're best friends."

What about those whose circle of friends contains no one suitable for or interested in coparenting? If they must look outside for a partner, how can they possibly assess those whom they contact? What criteria are important? Discussion with a number of successful coparents has established the elements central to compatible child-rearing:

1. **Similar philosophies about discipline and priorities.** In traditional marriages, conservative and casual attitudes tend to grow homogenous as the couple adapt to each other. With conscious coparenting, however, the relationship between adults is not the major motivation. It may be only marginal and there is less incentive to blend styles. Add to this the realistic assumption that

neither parent's style will dominate as strongly as in a straight family environment, and you can end up with confused kids. Additionally, the people who choose to become parents usually have a pretty clear idea of how they want to raise their children. Why take away from the joy of parenting by engaging in a philosophical battle between coparents? It is important to initially establish a set of behavioral guidelines for parent and child as well as to establish such priorities as home environments, schools, familial alliances, etc.

2. Financial responsibilities. Bringing a baby into the world is an expensive proposition. A major incentive to coparenting is sharing the financial burden. Whether this is split equally and literally between coparents or based on ability to contribute does not seem to be as important as having a clear-cut understanding about who is responsible for what.

At least one coparenting family contacted establishes financial contribution to child-raising by contributing a fixed percentage of each individual's income, with a minimum amount set to ensure that sufficient funds are available to meet the child's needs. Another family of three coparenting adults had a high dollar input from two of the parents while the third contributed full-time childcare until the child reached school age.

With the working woman currently earning only 59 percent of her male counterpart's salary, establishing "fair" or "equal" input may be difficult for a mixed-gender family. Even basing finances on a percentage of income is not truly fair when one party's overall earning potential is unfairly limited by our culture. The lesbian and gay coparents can only work for changing this double standard while following their conscience in their personal situation. Awareness of this potential inequity is helpful and clearly established agreements are vital.

3. Physical custody and living arrangements. Whatever their attitudes toward gay parenting, most child experts would agree that kids do best in a stable, secure environment. A responsible parent will attempt to provide such an environment. It is important, therefore, that potential coparents discuss the nature of their coparenting arrangement: do they share a single dwelling on a day-to-day basis or maintain separate homes, establishing a realistic and comfortable pattern of joint custody wherein the child spends a certain amount of time living with each parent?

Living together as friends, roommates or partners may be the simplest solution—if the parents are compatible and not heavily invested in another live-in relationship or into living alone. The logistics of a single residence in relationship to the child's school, friends, etc., are easier to manage. It is also cheaper since only one room and one set of furnishings, clothing and toys will be required for the child. Significant developments, vital information and good times can be directly experienced by both parents rather than as anecdotes told over the telephone.

It is important to remember too that very young babies (and they *all* start out that way!) pay little mind to parental schedules and preferences. They awaken at odd hours, fall sick with little warning and require constant supervision. The prospective parent must be aware of this; he or she needs to understand that parenting is hard work! Most of the labor is repetitious and not easily split task for task.

Practically speaking, coparents should seriously consider living together if the mother plans to breast-feed. This is one of those responsibilities that cannot realistically be split. (The exception would be if the other coparent is also a lactating woman—possible but not very likely). Breast-feeding is currently enjoying a resurgence of popularity in America. A 1984 survey indicated that more than half of all new mothers were choosing the breast over the bottle and the majority of by-choice mothers interviewed for this book had nursed their babies. It is difficult for partners to effect an equitable joint custody setup for a nursing newborn.

On the other hand, some coparents felt that their own need for independence and privacy outweighed the convenience of cohabitation (I use the term situationally, not sexually). Some had been single adults for so long that they did not believe that they could adapt to another adult in their home environment. Others opted for separate residences after the children were past infancy and somewhat independent of constant parental care. A third group saw advantages in separate homes in that this allows each partner time which is unbroken by the demands of parenting. These parents felt that the quality of attention and participation they gave their children outweighed the drawbacks of occasional separation. Generally, in two-household families, older children split their time between both households. The younger ones tended to remain with one or the other of the coparents a majority of the time, giving that individual primary physical custody. The distinction is made then between what English courts would call "care and control" (i.e., day-to-day responsibility for the child's well-being) and legal "custody," which involves parental rights over major decisions involving the child's upbringing and future. Thus, in some coparenting situations, one parent retains care and control while financial responsibility and general "custody" remain joint. Overall, custody in split-household coparenting is handled much like that in an amicable, cooperative divorce. The major difference is that, because the arrangement is private and not bound by a court order, greater flexibility is possible to adapt to the changing needs of parents and children.

4. Method of Conception. Even among those persons who have successfully sought and found a compatible parenting partner, the discussion regarding conception methods is apt to be a bit sticky. Parenting styles are easily debated and living arrangements are, as often as not, based on simple pragmatics. But the process of uniting sperm and egg in order to achieve fertilization is an intimate matter, something that many gay men and lesbians may not be comfortable talking about with one another.

We will assume, at this point, that criterion number 4 applies specifically to mixed-sex partners. Lesbians coparenting from conception will need to consult specific material in Chapter 9, "Artificial Insemination." Lesbians *and* gay men can refer to the sections on adoption. All of these chapters are relevant for both single parents and coparents.

"I just couldn't see conceiving my child with a turkey baster," says one lesbian coparent with a small chuckle. "It's perfectly fine for some women but I just didn't like the idea." She refers, of course, to do-it-yourself insemination, one of the techniques used to transfer sperm from coparent male to coparent female.

Insemination is the preferred method of those who wish to keep the coparenting relationship a pragmatic partnership, who find the idea of sexual intercourse with the prospective partner distasteful, uninteresting or simply unnecessary. It eliminates any concern about embarrassment, emotional complications and fear that uninspired coitus will not result in ejaculation. It appears to be as effective as the traditional method of fertilization. About 40 percent of the mixed-sex coparents contacted had used insemination.

Sexual intercourse was preferred when both partners felt comfortable with the act and with each other, were unaware of available alternatives or felt that the intimacy of intercourse was a significant part of the parenting bond, overriding any fear or personal awkwardness. They perceived it as an emotional and biological union toward a goal rather than a specifically sexual act. Generally those coparents who chose to conceive the "usual" way were already close friends and at ease with each other. They also had had some positive experience of heterosexual intercourse in their lives (though not necessarily with each other). One mother expressed her feeling thus:

"I felt it was important for both of us to make a baby; insemination just didn't seem an equal thing. And it helped Joel to know a little bit about how my body worked so he could understand the changes during pregnancy and be a part of that too. It wasn't a problem for us. It wasn't what we were used to but it was warm and friendly and we both felt good about it."

None of the parents who preferred intercourse had any regrets (nor for that matter did the insemination parents), and none of them felt that it had in any way changed their primary sexual orientation: each parent continued to identify himself or herself as gay or lesbian.

Whether you prefer to conceive through insemination or sexual intercourse, it needs to be discussed beforehand. Assumptions are dangerous and, not infrequently, the male needs a bit of educating about the female fertility cycle.

So, for that matter, do many women. (Refer to Chapter Nine for specifics in determining fertility.) No matter which method is used, timing is of the utmost importance to ensure conception. The old rule of thumb that a woman is ovulating (the ovum, or egg, is ready for fertilization by the sperm) fourteen days from the onset of her last menstrual period is extremely inaccurate. Ovulation can take place anytime during the cycle and the cycle itself varies from woman to woman—anywhere from twenty-six to thirty-five days in the normal female. When you consider that conception is possible for only a few days of this cycle it is easy to understand the need for accurate timing.

Relative to the above, it is also realistic to establish a maximum and a minimum time that the potential coparents will attempt conception. Nature can be obstinate; getting pregnant when you want to be is not the easiest thing in the world. It may occur after the first insemination or intercourse. It may take months. How long you are willing to wait and how many tries you find reasonable is a matter for personal discussion and clear understanding.

5. **Contracts.** The majority of heterosexual parents conceive their children while bound to the conventional contract of marriage. If that legal bond dissolves, they establish, through divorce proceedings, a new contract pertaining to the custody and care of their children. In many respects it's a haphazard system; a certain amount of responsibility is accorded each parent by legislation and tradition; the rest can go up in stormy debate during divorce.

Gay and lesbian coparents do not generally have the conventional protection and liability of marriage and so it is considered advisable for all parties to draw up, prior to conception, a legal contract detailing just what has been agreed upon, what is understood to be the responsibility of all parties, financial commitments, etc. Some contracts even appoint a guardian in the event of both parents' death.

As with other contracts discussed in this book, you are advised to consult an attorney experienced in lesbian and gay issues. (See the custody section in Chapter Eleven for specific advice on choosing a lawyer.) He or she can advise you of what rights and protections each of you are entitled to under the law and what precautions you can take to prevent controversy. One attorney consulted suggested that coparents appoint a third-party arbitrator to settle any future disputes. Some of the coparents felt that their best interests were served by having both father and mother retain separate lawyers to negotiate the contract. If there is no gay/lesbian advocate attorney in your area, you should at least retain a lawyer experienced in family law. Or contact the local chapter of the American Civil Liberties Union for advice.

Gay and Lesbian Couples as Coparents

Thus far, this chapter has addressed primarily gay men and lesbians choosing to coparent together. Many of the same considerations are valid for same-sex partners, particularly those whose bond is friendship rather than a love relationship. Same-sex coparents, however, face an additional dilemma: only one of the pair can be the child's biological parent and thus be ensured certain rights and responsibilities by law. The other partner(s) will have no legal relationship with the child and so special care must be taken to protect their rights as a parent.

Recently, in California, a suit was brought against a lesbian mother (who had conceived through artificial insemination) by her ex-lover, who stated that she had been as much a parent as the biological mother. With the breakup of the women's relationship, the nonbiological parent had been refused access to "her child." She sued for visitation privileges and was granted them in a preliminary hearing. The media coverage, though highly sensational, drew attention to the fact that there is no legal precedent for custody in same-sex coparenting situations. The courts had only heterosexual models to base their decisions on. Had this case come up in another area of the United States, it might never have reached the courts or been taken seriously; the nonbiological mother's claim might well have been written off as spurious. At the time of this writing, however, an order has been issued in Alameda County granting the nonbiological mother visitation rights and instructing her to make regular child-support payments. A breakthrough of no small importance has been made. Even the natural mother's attorney, a woman who has herself handled a number of lesbian custody cases with success, noted after the order was issued that the judge's decision was a significant step in the recognition of rights for lesbian mothers (and, by implication, gay fathers as well).

It seems, therefore, that for same-sex partners or in any case where only one coparent has a clear legal or biological claim to a child, a carefully written contract and good legal counsel is of utmost importance. No matter how sound and long-lived your relationship may seem, parenting changes people and prevention is far superior to pulling pieces back together after the dissolution of a relationship. For lesbians or gay men drafting a contract to cover coparenting situations through insemination or adoption, remember that only one of you will be the child's legal parent. In the event of a breakup, only the biological or adoptive parent will automatically have custody. A contract clause that plans for such an eventuality can save a great deal of expense and heartache later on. This is also true in the event of the biological/adoptive parent's death: your will(s) should provide for the other coparent to be appointed the child's guardian should this occur.

The old maxim about an ounce of prevention is a good one to bear in mind when getting into a coparenting relationship. Hope that you and your partner will stay on good terms forever, hope that you will both live to see your great-grandchildren playing on the lawn, but prepare for the possibility that neither of those things will come to pass. Far better to have a long and tedious legal contract moldering in a safe-deposit box than to have no clear-cut agreements at all and face a battle for the right to see your child.

All in all, coparenting is beginning to emerge as a significant alternative for lesbians and gay men. As more of us who have received the full impact of the gay liberation movement mature, we are standing up for our rights to reproduce, regardless of our affectional orientation. We are recognizing our ability to raise and nurture children as effectively as the heterosexual majority. But, learning from that majority, we see that the difficulties of raising children as single parents can be substantial and so we look for alternatives. Whether we parent as men together, women together or a cosexual unit, we learn, and therefore contribute something meaningful to our community: the joy and benefit of shared effort. By working together, we create a stronger future for ourselves and our children.

NINE

Lesbian Choices: Artificial Insemination

I'm going to be thirty soon. More and more I think that I'd like to have a child. We have that choice now.

SUZANNE, age twenty-nine

Until very recently, parenting was considered the exclusive prerogative of heterosexual couples, sanctioned by society only within the bounds of legal matrimony. To be sure, countless children have been born outside the institution of marriage, but both parents and children were made to feel the stigma. Childless heterosexual couples had one option if they wanted children: they could adopt. Since adoption in our modern culture involves considerable legal and financial resources, many couples could not exercise this option; their longing for a child remained unfulfilled. Then along came medical science with artificial insemination.

The idea is not really new. References to insemination with donated or purchased sperm exist in texts dating back to ancient Egypt and the Roman Empire. But the practice does not seem to have been widely practiced, nor were community resources for the screening and locating of potential donors available until the last couple of decades. Now the wonders of technology and the knowledge of genetics have evolved an elaborate system of fertility diagnosis, donor health screening and cryogenic (freezing) techniques which enable the donor semen to be quickly frozen and, when thawed, to remain alive.

For childless couples, the technique offered new hope, but only if failure to conceive was based upon the male partner's infertility. Artificial insemination cannot make a woman conceive if the problem stems from blocked fallopian tubes or failure to ovulate. Still, enough people were willing to explore artificial insemination that it became a real option and many childless couples knew the joy of parenthood.

Like parenting in general, artificial insemination by donor (hereafter referred to as AID) was considered an option available to heterosexual couples only. To this day most doctors will inseminate only a married woman who has explored all the usual routes of fertility testing, and then only with her husband's written consent. The donor is genetically selected to be as much like the "father" as possible. Single parenthood is considered "unhealthy" and not to be encouraged, a rather absurd notion considering the already enormous and still growing proportion of American households headed by single parents, usually women. If that woman is openly lesbian, many doctors will not even see her, much less agree to perform an insemination.

Gradually, however, in the wake of a growing number of single, apparently heterosexual women who have chosen to conceive through AID, the option of single-parenting or coparenting with a female partner is being exercised by lesbians who wish to have children but have no interest in entering into a physical relationship with a man. As a result of the close networking support systems that lesbian communities have evolved, information on AID has circulated and grown in scope and sophistication.

Today, lesbians using AID will discover that it has, in practice, moved outside the boundaries of mainstream medical jurisdiction and control. Most of the women I spoke to regarding their experience with AID conceived without the assistance of an M.D. (though most of them had had extensive health checkups and fertility tests). Often it was the woman's lover who had performed the actual insemination, at home, in the intimacy and warmth of personal surroundings.

"Some people think that artificial insemination is a cold, clinical procedure," says Sara, the lover of a woman who conceived through AID. "But they're wrong. I inseminated LeeAnn myself and it was the most intimate, beautiful act of love I have ever done."

The procedure involved in artificial insemination is simplicity itself. The woman to be inseminated lies in a supine position with her hips elevated. The fresh or thawed frozen semen is drawn slowly up into a syringe (without a needle, I hasten to add; special syringes are available for this). The syringe is inserted vaginally and directed to the top part of the woman's cervix. The plunger is pushed slowly, releasing the semen, then removed. That's it! All it takes is an ovulating woman, 1 cc of viable sperm, a cheap piece of equipment and some very basic knowledge of female anatomy. The latter two items are easily acquired; it is the first two which require thought, planning and, in some instances, a lot of work.

Fertility Awareness

A woman can be inseminated a hundred times with the healthiest semen available; if she does not ovulate while the sperm contained in that semen remain alive, she will never conceive. Our reproductive systems operate on a kind of timetable. Healthy, fertile women usually release one egg roughly every twenty-eight days. In order for conception to take place, live sperm must be present during the specific twelve-hour period that the egg is ready to be fertilized. Since sperm remains viable for three days at the most, timing is crucial in effective insemination.

The first step that must be taken by a woman who wants to conceive by AID is fertility awareness. She must be able to tell when she ovulates so that the insemination can coincide with her ovulation. The old rhythm method of contraception, in which you count fourteen days from the onset of menstrual flow and assume the onset of ovulation, is a crude version of fertility awareness. It is also highly inefficient, as many pregnant women have discovered to their surprise and chagrin. Every woman is different; the twenty-eight-day cycle with ovulation on the fourteenth day is only an average of the wide variety of patterns of a wide variety of bodies. The menstrual cycle can range from twenty to thirty-five days depending on the individual. Ovulation can take place at any time within that cycle—even during the menstrual flow itself. Only careful charting of body changes will determine what is normal for you.

There are many physical signs of ovulation, from midcycle cramping to changes in appetite and mood. Some women get many of them, some very few. The fertility-awareness methods currently being taught by holistic health centers across the country base their techniques on two or three signs common to *all* women:

1. **Changes in cervical mucus.** Both the consistency and the pH (acid-alkaline) balance of the mucus change as ovulation approaches and then gradually change back once it passes.
2. **Basal body temperature increase.** At ovulation, the body's basal temperature (which must be taken with a special thermometer that reads hundredths of a degree) rises at least .3 degree and then remains high until menstruation occurs.
3. **Changes in the cervix.** Both texture and position tend to change at ovulation.

These signs are noted on a graph over several months until a pattern appears and the woman learns to identify and predict her ovulation. Once this crucial period is established, the date(s) of insemination can be planned to coincide. For some women conception occurs quickly, sometimes after the very first insemination. Others take longer and many months pass before pregnancy occurs. Studies show that most women will conceive within twelve cycles of consistent inseminations.

Donors

Establishing fertility cycles and performing the actual insemination are basic steps. The real challenge of the AID issue is finding a suitable sperm donor. That may sound easy enough but the legal and emotional considerations surrounding this choice are many and complex. Everything from the health and genetic makeup of the sperm donor to the legal rights of both mother and donor must be examined carefully if future problems are to be avoided.

Lisa is a hospital dietitian with a four-year-old daughter conceived through AID. She had always wanted children and, when she turned thirty, decided it was time to get pregnant. Wanting to avoid the cost of a sperm bank, she put out feelers among her friends and acquaintances for a suitable donor. Don barely even qualified as an acquaintance, which was fine with Lisa; this was to be her child and she wasn't looking for a father. He was in good health and came well recommended. She asked him to be the donor; he agreed and they reached a verbal agreement: Don would donate the sperm necessary for Lisa to conceive. He would see the child once, after the birth. Other than that, he would have no involvement, no responsibilities of any sort; his name would not appear on the birth certificate. At the time, the arrangement appeared to suit everyone involved.

Now, five years later, Lisa is deeply enmeshed in a tangled court battle for custody of her daughter. Unknown to her, Don began announcing his impending "fatherhood" shortly after Megan's conception, though he was totally uninvolved with the pregnancy, planning or birth. He has decided that, verbal agreements not withstanding, he is Megan's "father" and entitled to joint custody of "his" child. The case has been ongoing for over three years and shows no sign of resolving itself with anything less than bitter resentment among all parties involved.

Lesbians who have had children through AID continually debate the issue of using a known donor versus one whose identity is unknown (or who does not know the mother). There are points to be made for both sides; much depends upon the mother's personal philosophy and preference. The legal system, as it exists today, has no precedents for the "rights" of lesbians conceiving through insemination. The idea is too new; the problems are unique and challenge the cherished notion of the two-parent (heterosexual) nuclear family being the "best" way to raise children. There is no way to predict which method (known versus unknown donor) is the legally "correct" way. Each court case that arises becomes a "test flight," eventually setting a precedent for the future. Today there is no certainty. As one attorney put it, "The only way to win is never to fight, never to end up in court."

I have talked to a number of women (single and couples) who have used AID. From their accounts of victories or frustrations I have attempted to present the points of view expressed by the majority regarding the selection of known or unknown donors and the benefits and potential liabilities of each.

Known Donors

There is a growing movement among adoptees to seek out and learn about their "natural" parents in order to better understand their social and genetic history. Some women, considering AID, wonder if this is not very likely to occur with their children when, one day, the child asks, "Who was my father?" With a known donor, this question can be easily answered, particularly if the donor is open to his identity's being revealed.

Medically, access to this information can be lifesaving. With transplants and tissue grafts on the increase, with many diseases revealed to be hereditary, the ability, in the future, to contact a donor and/or his family can provide crucial medical knowledge and potentially compatible donors of organs, tissue or bone marrow which can be obtained only from a blood relation. Should some question arise at a later date regarding the donor's family medical history, a known donor can be called upon to provide the needed information. Finally, a known donor is less likely to lie about his medical and family history, covering up some genetic predisposition to diseases such as diabetes or hemophilia. If he lies and a problem arises later, the known donor will have to face his lie, something that an unknown donor need not worry about.

The mother may desire that her child have contact with the biological "father." Many of the lesbians that I spoke with felt that it was a natural desire of children to know both parents and wanted someone who could provide some sort of male role model (though whether this is necessary or even desirable is a subject for fierce debate among lesbian mothers). Some women are not concerned with two-sex parenting, preferring to have and raise the child themselves or with a lover as a coparent, but more than a few felt that they would prefer some participation on the part of the donor.

Among those who made this choice, I found a wide range of donor involvement. The majority knew the donor only slightly but were on pleasant terms. The donors did not consider themselves fathers yet were willing to be available should some sort of crisis arise that required their input, such as the medical eventualities mentioned earlier. A few mothers were on friendlier terms with the donor and the men have spent occasional hours visiting the child, keeping in touch and following growth. The minority had close, warm relationships with their children's biological father. The mothers still retained custody and full parenting responsibilities but shared occasional weekends with the biological father, allowing their kids to grow up knowing him. This situation is still far from coparenting, but it retains an almost polar distinction from the desires and attitudes of women who chose to use sperm from an unknown donor.

The greatest concern involving a known donor is illustrated by Lisa's dilemma: what if the "donor" suddenly changes his mind and wants to be a "father"? Suddenly, there is someone vying with the mother for the child's time, for the right to guide and raise the child. If the donor knows the mother, is a local individual and is not bound, prior to entering the project, by a clearly defined legal document stating that the mother is the sole and final responsible parent, many women fear interference with a carefully planned life-style. Even with a legal contract, a man who chooses to involve himself in a child's life may be looked upon with favor by the patriarchal judicial system and given "rights" (which he had previously given up) by a court which has no experience with lesbian mothers. This is particularly true if the donor is a heterosexual male. With a lesbian mother and a straight "father," it remains too likely that the father will win out in court. For this reason, many women choosing a known donor seek him among their gay male acquaintances. They reason that if both parents are homosexual, that cannot become an issue in court.

With the emergence of acquired immune deficiency syndrome (AIDS), however, the suitability of gay men as sperm donors has come into question. In February 1984, the Northern California Sperm Bank, which supplies many lesbians with sperm for self-insemination, reluctantly decided to stop accepting gay male donors until more is known about AIDS detection and prevention. In a recent gay and lesbian parenting conference, the issue of AIDS was a major topic of discussion. It was of enough concern to warrant separate research. The issue of sperm donation and AIDS is discussed at length in Chapter Seven.

One lesbian couple came up with a unique and interesting selection of a donor. The partner who was not going to conceive asked her brother to donate semen. The brother was close to the couple and very supportive. Though he had no desire to take an active parenting role, he was more than willing to help them in their wish to have a child. The women's son is therefore related to the lover by blood as well as love. He is genetically as close to both of his mothers as possible and everyone involved is very happy with the arrangement.

Another couple inseminated with sperm donated by a male friend who lives across the country from them. They were fortunate enough to conceive during the brief period he was visiting their town. Again, this friend was not particularly interested in an active parenting role but happily supported his friends in their goals. He sees his daughter occasionally, enjoying the visits, but is content to remain mostly uninvolved.

Overall, the women who have had pleasant experiences with known donors selected friends, men whom they had known for some time and whose attitudes and integrity they were fairly well assured of. Choosing a donor from among casual acquaintances or friends of friends did not seem to work quite as well: too often both parties, without friendship as incentive, reverted to selfish and inconsiderate behavior or failed to communicate clearly and ended tangled up in misunderstandings. As with all areas of planned parenting, no amount of afterthought can compensate for inadequate preparation.

Multiple Donors

A rather creative alternative to the known-donor dilemma is using sperm obtained from multiple donors, who are aware that the mother is inseminating with several men's sperm simultaneously. It eliminates certainty on the part of any one man that the child in question is actually his while allowing the mother to review and screen her donors more directly. It has also been used as a clever ruse.

Kimberly laughs when asked why she chose the multiple-donor option.

"I wanted to know who the father is," she admits readily, "but I didn't want *him* to know and possibly get his ego involved with *my* child. See, I really did get sperm from five different men who knew about the insemination, but I actually only used the one I really felt was the best genetic material. None of them know that, though, and so I feel pretty secure."

There are, of course, a few weaknesses in this system. If the child turns out to bear a striking resemblance to one of the men, the uncertainty can be eliminated. There are blood tests available today that can determine whether a man and child are genetically related to about 96 percent accuracy. If the known donors continue to have contact with mother and/or child there is some potential for future interference. The possibility cannot be overlooked, though such complications have not, to the best of my sources' knowledge, arisen at the present time.

The other difficulty is finding a number of suitable donors. Of course, if you really are only using the multiple-donor fiction as a smoke screen, all you need is one genuinely suitable donor and two or three more who are simply cooperative. Some women will find this all quite manageable, some will have trouble finding even that one acceptable donor and some have reservations about perpetuating a fiction.

As with a single known donor, it might be wise to have written agreements drawn up between mother and all parties in a multiple-donor situation.

Agreements and Contracts

One experienced lesbian lawyer I spoke to put her attitude toward mother-donor contracts quite concisely:

"A contract isn't a guarantee that you will win in court. Even the best contract can be got around. What that piece of paper does do is discourage litigation. Most people won't change their minds if they know they've signed a legal contract. A written agreement states intent. It serves as an indicator of what both parties had in mind when it was drawn up. Therefore, the more detailed and thorough the document, the better."

The enforceability of contracts between a woman and a sperm donor has not been put to much of a test. It is unknown at this time how legally binding they are. Nonetheless, every lawyer I spoke with regarding lesbian insemination felt that a signed agreement was strongly advisable. As more and more lesbians choose to parent through self-insemination, there will be more opportunities for contention and controversy to arise. A document that is signed by both parties and clearly states their intent may prevent disastrous litigation at a future date. Obviously each case will be unique and each agreement tailored to fit the needs of the individuals involved.

If you intend to inseminate using donor sperm from a known party, please consult an attorney first. (See the custody section in Chapter Eleven for recommendations on selecting a competent lawyer.) If there are no attorneys in your area who have experience with this sort of contract, do your best to find one who is at least sympathetic and willing to learn what is required. A very useful and informative paper is available from the Lesbian Rights Project, 1370 Mission Street, 4th floor, San Francisco, CA 94103. Written by Donna Hitchens, it is entitled *Lesbians Choosing Motherhood: Legal Issues in Donor Insemination.* It not only goes into the various legal ramifications of insemination but includes some sample contracts and agreements.

Unknown Donors

The overwhelming benefit of using sperm from an unknown donor is that it prevents the sort of dilemma that Lisa has been experiencing—that of the donor attempting to obtain the legal rights of a father against the wishes and plans of the mother. Obviously such interference can occur only if the donor knows the identity of the woman using his sperm. With unknown donors it is almost impossible for such a situation to arise. There are, however, other potential problems and considerations.

The woman choosing to conceive with sperm from an anonymous donor has several options: she can obtain the semen and/or be inseminated through a physician or sperm bank, or she can find someone to serve as a go-between, locating a suitable donor and arranging to get the fresh semen while keeping the identities of both parties confidential. Let's examine both options.

Physician or Sperm Bank. The primary advantage of these resources is complete and legally sound anonymity for all parties involved. The donor has already signed away all rights and responsibilities and the legal system generally recognizes those contracts as valid. Presumably the donor has been screened for significant medical problems, though you can't always count on this: the word of the donor on family and personal history is all that anyone really has to go on. Additionally, you have a choice of different physical types to choose from, which may not always be possible when looking at acceptable known donors.

The drawbacks are substantial enough to have triggered an "underground" insemination movement over the last several years. The impersonal atmosphere of insemination in a doctor's office can turn some people off. The physician or clinic may ask extensive questions about why you are choosing insemination and they may refuse to inseminate single women, particularly if they are lesbians. Also, you have no access to the donor's family medical history should your child become ill and need additional information at some time in the future. Finally, doctors and clinics are expensive. If it takes several months for you to conceive, the cost can run into the hundreds, even thousands, of dollars for insemination alone.

Using a physician or sperm bank seems to be the best course for women who live in an area with access to a feminist- or lesbian-run facility that will be supportive and ask few questions about your motive, those for whom the cost factor is not crucial, and those for whom the single most important factor is a guarantee of anonymity.

Go-Betweens. The position of a go-between in artificial insemination by an unknown donor is one of real responsibility. The go-between must be trusted to seek out and find a donor who meets the prospective mother's specifications, is medically sound and, above all, is willing to participate. The go-between must arrange for any documents or contracts to be executed, see that sperm is delivered to the right place at the right time and, finally, be able to keep the identities of both parties completely confidential.

If you know someone who is trustworthy enough to assume this responsibility and is willing to do so, you have one of the best possible balances between anonymity and personal control over your insemination. The potential is there for a well-executed agreement that will enable you to determine the donor's identity at some time in the future if a medical crisis arises (this should be clearly defined in your contract.) You have the means to self-inseminate at home, and you retain your anonymity.

Potential problems are that the go-between may not retain the same right of confidentiality that a physician does. If subpoenaed by a court of law, he or she could possibly be forced to reveal the identities of one party or other. In a few states it is illegal to self-inseminate and, while you may be willing to take on the risk yourself, you are also placing the go-between in danger of criminal prosecution. Finally, if the go-between is not as trustworthy as expected, critical identifying information could be leaked out in the future. A written, notarized agreement between the involved parties and the go-between is therefore recommended.

Using an unknown donor, whichever source you choose, gives the benefits of anonymity. Because you cannot expect to determine the donor's identity, it is recommended that you carefully screen your source to be sure that it is reliable, legal and thorough in its screening of donors. Read any and all documents thoroughly before you sign them and, if there is any doubt, check with an experienced attorney for advice.

TEN

Adoption and Foster Parenting

In January 1983 David Frater, an openly gay man from Riverside, California, made national news when he adopted seventeen-year-old Kevin. The boy, who had been living with Frater for two years as a foster child, identifies himself as heterosexual.

This was not the first time that a homosexual has adopted a child, but it is one of the first well-publicized instances in which the adoptive parent was known to be gay and still won legal custody of a minor child. It was an important victory for David Frater and for the many lesbians and gay men who would like to follow suit and adopt children of their own without feeling pressured to hide their sexual orientation.

In the course of our research, we found that adoptive parents were far and away the most reluctant to identify themselves and/or be interviewed. Many people mentioned to us that they knew of gay men or lesbians who had successfully adopted children, yet when approached, few of those parents were willing to even complete questionnaires. They had invested much energy into playing down their homosexual orientation during the adoption process and were not willing to risk public disclosure, even with a guarantee of anonymity. The very few adoptive parents who would talk to me also emphasized the need for privacy. Like any case in which custody has been granted through the legal process, an adoptive parent's suitability can be brought into question at any time. Having gone through the system once, no one wants to repeat the process.

Social service agencies were also reticent, though for different reasons. Most agencies, whether county, state or private, are legally barred from discussing the details of adoption cases. Furthermore, there is no established procedure for assessing gay adoptions. Each case is unique. There is little precedent and certainly there are no statistics available for the lesbian or gay man who wishes to adopt. It is difficult, from the cut-and-dried responses, to determine if homosexuality alone would make any given agency reject a potential parent out of hand. Certainly none of the agencies sounded particularly enthusiastic about the prospect of having gay applicants.

On the other hand, several agencies now place gay youths in gay foster homes, particularly when the child has had repeated difficulties in heterosexual foster homes because of her or his homosexuality. Several of the parents who did agree to talk to us began as foster parents, finding it the easiest way to get the ball rolling on adoptions.

Larry and Beth are married and live in rural Tennessee. Beth is a lesbian activist whose construction job provides the income for their family. Larry has known he was gay since childhood, is totally accepting of it and is the domestic half of the marriage, working at home as a househusband. They have adopted two boys and a girl who first came to them as foster children.

"The hardest thing about our particular parenting hasn't had to do with our being gay," says Larry. "It has to do with society's racism because my children are black . . . which has been hard for us because that's a visible difference." These two appear to have worked with an important opening in the system: they adopted older black children, traditionally hard to place in a permanent home. "It's easier to get biracial kids once you're a biracial family; the social workers are trying to place those kids . . . After bringing the first biracial kid into our family, it's become easier to adopt."

Although gay men, lesbians and single heterosexuals continue to press for adoptions, the truth remains that the children considered most "desirable" (i.e., healthy white infants) tend to be placed first with that bastion of American normalcy, heterosexual Caucasian couples with above-average incomes. Gays and singles have a much better chance of adopting if they are willing to accept the "hard-to-place" kids—older, minority or handicapped children whose needs and personalities are already established. Social service agencies are eager to place the difficult children, some of whom are emotionally fragile after an unsuccessful string of foster homes, and they are much more likely to turn a blind eye to marital status and/or sexual orientation when screening potential parents.

A spokesman for the National Association of Social Workers' committee on homosexual issues states that his organization assumes a position of encouraging full adoption rights for gays. There is a long-standing precedent for placing homosexual foster children in gay households and the adoption issue is viewed as a logical extension of foster care policies. Membership in or familiarity with this national association and its policy would seem to be a plus when choosing a social service or adoption agency. Bulletins and statements from the NASW or the American Psychological Association (which also favors gay foster care) cannot hurt a would-be parent in reasoning with officials in adoption matters.

It would also seem that having family support is helpful in establishing suitability as an adoptive parent. Most of those we talked to had some form of close family available to help with child-rearing. Larry and Beth, while unquestionably gay, are married; they are close friends and helpmates. David Frater and son Kevin live with David's mother as a family unit. Other lesbian and gay adoptive parents have their own, supportive families living nearby, interacting with the kids and helping to lighten the load of responsibility.

"My mother is very supportive," Beth comments. "My family is confused about how we've chosen to be parents, confused because it challenges a lot of their stereotypes . . . . Confused as they may be, they're proud of us, love the kids, and support us."

On the other hand, Larry tells us, "My mother doesn't speak to me. Not because I'm gay necessarily, but because the kids are black . . . because I got married, she didn't have to think about whether I was gay."

It seems clear that bias still exists, from courts, placement agencies and even from families; what is acceptable to one faction may be unpalatable to another. The would-be parent needs to tread carefully among many considerations when adoption is the issue. For some of us, the secrecy and the limitations imposed are more than we are willing to take on. Others run up against prejudice within the system, harassment, excessive screening and long delays. Yet we persevere and continue to prove that being gay is not implicitly a barrier to adoption. Those who have succeeded appear to have no regrets; most of us feel that we have chosen the best possible route: mature and intentional parenthood. Says Larry: "I'm scandalized that people could be anything other than 'intentional parents' because it's too much of a commitment over too long a time to be able to do it justice unless you choose it . . . You can't take the attitude that you got mugged into having a child."

Another option available to the potential adoptive parent is a private or contractual adoption. This procedure, by which the adoptive parent makes private arrangements with a pregnant woman to adopt her child at birth, is legal in varying degrees around the country.

Carol and Delores live in California and have been lovers for many years. In June 1984, they adopted a baby boy. When asked if they went through one of the county adoption agencies, Carol laughed cynically and shook her head. "Are you kidding?" she asked. "We're an interracial lesbian couple. They didn't want anything to do with us!" Their private adoption, by direct arrangement with the baby's natural mother, went through smoothly and quickly. They are ecstatic with their son and pleased with the private adoption process.

Commonly, the adoptive parent agrees to pay for the expenses surrounding the mother's pregnancy and may additionally support her during that period, as well as covering legal fees. This is an expensive proposition. Maternity costs range from $2,000 to $5,000 for a normal, uncomplicated delivery; they are much higher if the child is delivered by C-section or the baby has health problems at birth. Legal fees too vary widely; a friendly gay-oriented attorney may charge only a moderate fee plus filing costs, another lawyer many thousands of dollars. Support for the expectant mother further inflates expenses, and, finally, if a private agency is utilized to contact a potential mother and screen the parent (required by law in some states), there will be a considerable agency fee.

The advantages of private adoption are obvious, particularly in those states that allow individuals to independently contract with expectant mothers (or their guardians in the case of pregnant minors) without too much intervention by state agencies. If the potential parent has adequate income, decent housing and a history of stability, the screening process need never touch on the subject of sexual orientation and the would-be parent need not hide anything or hedge about his or her private life. If the mother is an acquaintance or family member (which is not uncommon) and already knows about the adoptive parent's orientation, so much the better. Don't forget, however, that even a private adoption must be approved by a judge. Arranging to adopt a child through private agencies or attorneys may simplify the process somewhat but won't eliminate it entirely.

The primary drawback in gay adoption is that only one of the partners in a relationship may legally adopt the child. The other partner's legal relationship with the child is tenuous. This is much like the status of the nonbiological lesbian mother in cases of artificial insemination, and the same precautions and careful contracts are recommended to protect both partners' rights in the event the relationship breaks up.

As with most other areas involving gays and the legal system, prospective adoptive parents should be cautious. Find yourself a good lawyer, preferably one who has handled similar cases successfully in the past. (Suggestions on selecting an attorney can be found in Chapter Eleven in the custody section.) Before you even walk into a lawyer's office, know exactly what it is you want (infant, older child, contract adoption), how much you can afford to spend on medical, agency and legal fees, and what concessions you are willing to make in order to become an adoptive parent.

Foster Parenting

Those who, for one reason or another, opt not to invest eighteen or twenty years in a child's birth, growth and development, yet are interested in providing nurturing and guidance to a child, may find their niche in foster-parenting programs. Foster parents provide homes, help and love to young people on a temporary basis (anywhere from three months to many years). The children remain wards of the state during this time and, in most cases, the foster parent is allotted funds to cover the child's expenses. Often the objective is to provide a home environment and parental type of discipline for children whose own parents are unable to care for them. In many cases, the goal is to ultimately return the kids to their own families should this prove feasible. Sometimes adoption is possible in the long run, though this is not generally the goal in foster care.

What is true of adoption is even more true of foster parenting: the greatest need is for homes for older, minority and handicapped children. Poverty and child abuse contribute to the overwhelming majority of cases; some of these kids have never had a stable environment in their short lives.

A popular misconception is that teenagers in need of foster homes are all juvenile delinquents—unmanageables, drug abusers, problem children. Indeed, many of these kids have reached the social service agencies through the juvenile division of the criminal justice systems but, more often than not, they are victims, not criminals. Often they are runaways. Some of them have been involved with drugs or prostitution or petty crime, but these are symptoms of the real problems—abuse (physical and sexual), desperate poverty, rejection.

Some of them have done nothing worse than tell their parents that they are gay. Since the late sixties, social service agencies in major cities have become aware of the problems of gay teenage runaways. These kids have been thrown out or severely punished for their orientation. They make their way to cities like New York or San Francisco, hoping to find acceptance and a chance to make it on the streets. Some of them are scarred—physically and emotionally—unable to accept themselves, unable to live in an environment that scorns and hates what they are. There are young lesbians from rural areas who have been sexually abused by older family members in a sick effort to "straighten them out," young boys forced to leave home and prostitute themselves because they are young and gay and have no place to turn. The problems with placing such kids in a homophobic world are enormous. Foster homes which accept a variety of children may be unable to cope with the homosexual teen. In some areas the withdrawn, retarded or hostile teen may be much easier to place in a foster home than a cheerful, cooperative gay.

Some states have begun placing gay kids in gay foster homes. New Jersey gained some publicity for this practice, though it is not (according to social service representatives) an "official" policy. The main concern reflects back on gay parenting overall: are gays acceptable parents, biologically or otherwise? Many jurisdictions (meaning the social workers and agencies therein) still say no. Others have overcome cultural conditioning and established their criteria for foster parenting on the basis of the individual's qualifications as a stable person. They may not even be aware of the foster parent's orientation. Until fairly recently, there has been little attempt to accept gay foster parents and match them up with young gays in need of supportive, understanding homes.

Yet there is a need for such homes. Each year thousands of children from infancy on require temporary shelter. Some of them wind up in institutionalized settings because there is no room for them elsewhere. Others turn to the streets, where they become targets for pimps, heroin dealers and psychopaths. Only about 10 percent of those in their teens are able to return home, problems resolved. Currently there are dozens of children for every foster home that becomes available.

The criteria for being licensed as a foster home vary from jurisdiction to jurisdiction. Sexual orientation may be a prohibiting factor or it may be considered totally irrelevant. Some states may not accept you if they know that you are gay, but they will never *ask* you directly and it becomes an issue only if you or someone else informs them. Overall, the traits sought are stability in job, community and mentality, sufficient home space to adequately house a child or children, and abilities in support and nurture. If you believe that you have these qualities to offer a child and could handle the temporary nature of the placements, kids need your help.

ELEVEN

Custody, Visitation and Guardianships

Of all the challenges faced by lesbian and gay parents in a heterosexist society, the fight to obtain custody of children following divorce is probably the most painful and the most widely publicized.

"Lesbian Mother Reportedly Given Custody of Child" reads one caption in the Louisville *Times.* "Homosexual Father Awarded Custody of Twins" another Midwestern paper announces. Across the United States, the public is becoming aware that gay fathers and lesbian mothers are asserting their right to raise children.

What the papers don't report are the stories of hundreds of men and women who lose their court battles, the thousands whose sexuality never comes up in court and yet influences their decision whether or not to seek custody. Only when a gay parent goes to court and wins is the case considered news.

"Don't even bother fighting," a lawyer told a Texas father recently when the man acknowledged that he was gay. "You don't stand a chance and it'll just be a waste of time and money." For many years this was the stock response of attorneys faced with a parent's homosexuality. The odds of a positive outcome seemed so low that lawyers concentrated on visitation rights and alimony payments.

Happily, things are looking up. Although there are no reliable statistics available to determine the exact percentage of gay and lesbian parents awarded custody of their kids, there are indications that the number is rising. News columns in such gay publications as *The Advocate* are carrying stories about court victories with increasing frequency. Attorneys committed to gay and lesbian issues affirm that, slowly and gradually, progress is being made. The parent who chooses to take the fight to court still faces an uphill struggle, but it is no longer an impossible one.

Girding for Battle

Today, an increasing number of states are adopting simplified no-fault divorce procedures that are geared to facilitate the dissolution of marriages with a minimum of red tape. That is, provided that there are no children. When the divorcing couple has children, simplified divorce is no longer quite so simple. In most states there will automatically be a custody hearing to determine which parent (or both) should have custody of the kids. Even when there is no disagreement between the divorcing partners, a custody hearing is usually required. If the partners present a written stipulation to the judge at this time, detailing an arrangement both have agreed on, they can usually (but not always) relieve much of the expense and strain. Most responsible attorneys will encourage their clients to try to come to an agreement with the ex-spouse that is acceptable to both rather than encouraging long and costly litigation.

People undergoing a divorce are not always reasonable, however. The pain of a failed marriage rarely brings out the best in partners and, when a spouse's homosexuality is a contributing factor, upset frequently explodes into outright hostility. At this stage getting an acceptable compromise on custody may not be possible. The gay parent must be prepared to accept that a custody struggle may well follow on the heels of divorce.

If you have decided that you do indeed want either sole or joint custody of your child or children, you must next ask yourself if you are prepared to fight for it. This means a lot more than simply hiring a competent attorney and paying her or him to handle it for you. For the homosexual parent it probably means having your life-style, your relationships, your children and your activities scrutinized by strangers, some of whom will probably be most unsympathetic. After the scrutiny, the information and conjectures gleaned will be paraded in a public courtroom. You will be asked all manner of personal questions, some relevant to your parenting ability, some asked out of ignorance, bigotry or prurience. You and your children may undergo a battery of psychological tests and, above all, you will be out of your closet for good if the subject of homosexuality is allowed as admissible evidence in court. It is important to decide whether you have the stamina to cope with a struggle that could be drawn out over many months or even years. This means a realistic examination of yourself, your support systems and your environment. If, after analyzing these things, you decide that you do want to take the issue to court, the next step is hiring an attorney to represent you.

Choosing a Lawyer

It is of utmost importance that you find a lawyer you feel comfortable with and whom you trust to look out for your interests. During the months of litigation you are going to be putting your future and your children's future in his or her hands. If you do not feel at ease in discussing your circumstances and history with your attorney, a potentially stressful situation can become a full-blown nightmare. Therefore, if you, like most of us, don't already have an attorney who is familiar with the ins and outs of gay parent custody litigation, you are going to need to shop around. *Don't* be afraid to consult several lawyers before making your decision. Many good lawyers offer a free or low-cost initial consultation. A reputable lawyer is going to be just as concerned as you are about whether or not he or she can properly represent your case. Your lawyer wants to check you out too. Even if all your initial consultations involve a small fee, it's worth it to get the best possible counsel on your case.

Don't hire a lawyer who enthusiastically guarantees that she or he can win the case for you. Any lawyer experienced in this type of litigation knows that it's a difficult situation and will advise you of that. *Do* contact local support groups, gay and women's service organizations and national organizations such as the local chapter of the American Civil Liberties Union in your area for referrals. Many of them can provide referrals to local attorneys experienced with situations like yours. The Resources section of this book lists a number of individuals and organizations that provide referrals.

Do feel free to ask the attorney about his or her feelings regarding homosexuality and parenting. Remember that there are homophobic lawyers too. Just because they are interested in your case as a civil rights issue doesn't mean that they are free of bias. Attorneys who are not comfortable with homosexual issues or people, or who harbor negative attitudes, are not going to be able to do their best to represent you. *Do* take the lawyer's sex into account. A lesbian lawyer may be no more comfortable with a gay father than her heterosexual counterparts and vice versa. Also, be clear about your own feelings. Most of us genuinely want to overcome sex biases but—let's be honest—many of us are going to be most comfortable and open with a lawyer of our own sex. Sex probably shouldn't be the main consideration in your selection, but any prejudices you or they might have regarding sex need to be taken into account.

Do discuss fees. For most of us, the cost of custody litigation is a major concern and rightly so. Legal costs run high, particularly when the case drags out or has to be appealed. Few lawyers are able or willing to quote a flat dollar fee at the time of the initial interview, but they should be able to give you an idea of their fee scale and what sort of arrangements they will consider for payments. Your lawyer should also be willing to present you with an itemized bill, detailing all costs incurred. If he or she isn't willing to discuss the cost factor or demands payment up front, he or she is probably not the lawyer for you.

Don't be scared away from a good lawyer because of the fee. If the estimate is more than you think you can afford to finance, try to negotiate. If you feel that the fee is reasonable but still more than you can realistically manage (and lawyers' fees *are* high in this type of case), check with your local support groups and such organizations as NOW (the National Organization for Women). There are ways to raise funds for custody cases like yours and many organizations are experienced in this and willing to help.

The National Gay Task Force has put together a support packet for gay and lesbian parents. The following checklist (and others used in this chapter) are reprinted here by permission.

Questions to Ask a Lawyer Before Hiring

1. (Over the phone.) Is there an initial consultation fee? If so, how much?
2. Do you have experience with child custody cases? With lesbians? With gay men? With gay custody cases? How many cases like mine have you handled? How did they turn out?
3. Do you have any special expertise that will be helpful in handling my case?
4. Do you have any doubts about lesbian mothers or gay fathers raising children?
5. Are you familiar with the special strategy problems involved in a lesbian/gay custody case (personal/political decisions like whether to admit being gay, whether to live with a lover, etc.)?
6. Are you willing to accept help from gay groups that can offer resources (sample decisions/opinions, articles, etc.)?
7. What are your office procedures? When can you be reached? What about weekends and evenings? How will we stay in touch as the case proceeds?
8. Will you consult with me before making any decisions in the case? Will you keep me informed of anything that happens?
9. Who will be doing most of the work on my case (you or an

assistant)? Will you consult with another attorney? Can I meet the people who will be involved in my case?

10. How long do you expect this case to take? Will you prepare an estimated timetable for the case?

11. What are your fees? Will you write out an estimate of the costs of the case?

12. When do you want to be paid? Will you supply an itemized bill when the case is over?

Things to Keep in Mind After You've Hired a Lawyer

Question any changes in strategy or deviations from the estimated bill and timetable. You should be involved in any decisions to change plans.

Get copies of or look over all correspondence and court documents in the case.

Your lawyers should keep you informed about the progress of the case and give you frequent progress reports.

Make sure you thoroughly understand what is happening and that you get information to make reasoned decisions about your case.

If you have problems with your lawyer, you may want to consult with another lawyer. If you do decide to get another lawyer, some things to remember:

Try to line up another lawyer before you fire the first, so you don't get caught without a lawyer if something comes up suddenly.

Make sure you get back all the correspondence and other papers. The lawyer may try to hold on to your file until you pay your bill, and you may have to negotiate about how much of the bill you owe. Your new lawyer may be useful in resolving any disputes.

Although it may not be possible to get a lawyer with experience handling gay and lesbian custody cases in every area, these guidelines should help you in obtaining the best legal counsel available. Don't underestimate the need for a good attorney; as a lesbian or gay man facing our legal system, you are going to need the best representation you can get.

Deciding What Type of Custody You Want

Once you have an attorney, the two of you will have to sit down and decide precisely what it is you are after. Depending on which state you live in, there are several types of custody and it's important to have a clear idea of what degree of legal responsibility you want for your child. You should probably have this firmly in mind before your initial interview; that way the attorney can advise you as to just what you're up against.

Legal Custody and Physical Custody

A parent with *legal custody* of a child has legal rights and responsibilities for major decisions concerning the child's well-being and care. This would include schooling, medical care, social environment, etc. *Physical custody* means that the child lives with you a majority of the time. Many people assume that these two go hand in hand and they usually do. However, it is possible for both parents to share legal custody while only one parent is the custodial parent (with physical custody). This is not a wholly unusual arrangement when both parents are equally committed to their child's welfare but unamenable to sharing physical custody. It may be an option available to you and may help make an ex-spouse more agreeable to your having physical custody. Problems occur when your relationship with the other parent is not cooperative, a common state of affairs during divorce. It may be unrealistic to expect that the two of you can agree on crucial issues in the future. Sharing legal custody should be reserved for those situations where both partners have shown a willingness to cooperate on child-rearing issues, regardless of whom the child lives with.

Joint Custody

This arrangement, whereby two parents share legal and physical custody on a fairly even basis, is becoming more common as both parents take a keener interest in child-rearing. Some states, such as California, are assuming that joint custody is best when the parents are agreeable (or even when only one parent is agreeable). They base this assumption on findings that children benefit from maximum contact with both parents. Joint custody, if it is available where you live, may be a reasonable compromise between you and your former partner. There are many ways to arrange this: some parents alternate days or weeks, others prefer greater consistency, with one parent having the child during the school year and the other during vacations for a fixed period, then switching this around so that the other parent has school-year custody.

Joint custody does ensure that your child or children will have contact with both you and their other parent. It is also very demanding on you. It requires that you maintain contact with your ex-partner and cooperate on major decisions on a regular basis, and, in most cases, it limits your ability to move more than an easy car ride away from your former spouse. In the case of gay and lesbian parents, there is also the concern about what a hostile ex is telling the children about you during his or her time with them. Consistency is important to kids. If you don't think that you and your former partner can maintain consistency and communication then joint custody is not the solution for you.

Split Custody

Split custody is when each parent has physical custody of one or more children. Judges are very reluctant to agree to split custody. Generally this occurs only when each child has been living with a different parent for a significant length of time already and is happy with the arrangement. It is also found in cases of older (teenage) children who were permitted to choose which parent they wanted to live with. Splitting siblings can be extremely traumatic and is not a step to be taken lightly. Even if you and your ex-spouse come to an agreement on this, it may take some doing to persuade the judge that this is the best solution. Split custody is not perceived to be in the best interests of the children.

Preparing for Your Case

Once you and your attorney know what you are after, she or he will probably start researching similar cases in your area. Your particular circumstances are going to be instrumental in determining the approach your lawyer will take in court and you should expect to answer quite a few questions about yourself, your children and your involvements at this point. In the Gay Parent's Support Packet, the National Gay Task Force has included a checklist of issues to be considered by you and your lawyer prior to preparing your case. The issues they raise for you to consider are:

1. Are you seeking personal support to give you strength before, during and after the trial?

2. Have you really thought through the decision of custody versus visitation versus split custody?

3. If you don't have custody of your child before the trial, spend as much time as possible with her or him.

4. If you don't believe anyone knows about your being gay, how certain are you? I.e., Do you live with your lover? Go to the bars?

5. Have you made a conscious decision about continuing to live with or moving in with your lover?

6. Do you feel that you and your lover can get through the trial and still have positive feelings toward each other? How will you deal with bad feelings?

7. Have you been able to be honest with your lawyer about past legal or psychological problems? Anything on record can be found out. How about your child?

8. Can you write out your philosophy of child-rearing and how you implement it with your own children? Include a daily time schedule of how you and your child or children spend the day, especially how much time is spent together.

9. What does your child know about your being gay? Are her or his feelings positive? Can negative feelings be dealt with?

10. How does your child deal with your lesbian or gay identity in relation to his or her friends and relatives?

11. How does your child identify her or his sexuality?

12. If the judge asks you how you feel about your child or children's sexual/affectional preference, will you be prepared to answer this question?

13. Realistically assess your child or children's relationship to your lover (if applicable).

14. Is your child around any role models of the opposite sex?

15. Have you considered having an attorney represent your child?

16. Be prepared to answer the questions "Who would you choose, between your lover and your child or children?" "How often do you and your lover sleep together?" "What do you do?" (The strategy that you and your lawyer should use, though, is to have an expert witness discuss these matters, not you.)

17. How long are you willing to drag out the settlement decision in an effort to stay out of court?

18. What limitations on your political and personal activities are you willing to accept?

19. Are you prepared to make a conventional appearance for both your child and yourself? I.e., clothes, hair, etc.

20. Do you understand your spouse's motives for wanting custody?

21. Is there any possibility that your spouse has been involved in a gay or adulterous relationship?

"The Best Interests of the Children"

In many places the phrase "In the best interests of the children" is the sole guideline given to judges to help them decide which parent should have custody. Unfortunately, nobody knows exactly what the best interests of the children really are and that uncertainty can weigh heavily against a lesbian or gay parent. The average judge is a white heterosexual male. You may end up with a judge who happens to be a black lesbian, but I wouldn't count on it, even in the most enlightened metropolis. What a straight white man of fifty considers to be "best" for a child is based on his experience and prejudices. Yes, a judge is supposed to be above prejudice when rendering a decision but homophobia is so deeply ingrained that even a reasonable official will probably see his homophobic expectations as "facts." One of the key aspects, then, of presenting a lesbian or gay custody case, is going to be educating the judge about homosexuality and doing it in a nonthreatening way.

Before you go any further, you had better examine yourself and your motivations. *Why* do you want custody? Do you honestly feel that you would be the better parent to raise your child? Have you been the primary parent up until now? Are *you* the one willing to compromise on joint custody? Does your child want to live with you? Or are you seeking custody in order to get revenge on your ex-spouse? If you answered yes to that last question, drop your case right now. When getting even or hurting a former partner is the motivation for seeking custody, it is the children who suffer most. They are being used as pawns in a power game played by hostile adults and the effect of this can be devastating.

The revenge motive is more commonly seen in the ex-spouse of a gay parent. Discovering that one's partner is homosexual can be a real blow to a person's ego and confidence. In the anger that often results, many people are not above using the children to get even. I know of several people (all of them women, incidentally) who lost custody of their children to a hostile spouse. Then, after a period of months or years, the ex suddenly showed up at the door saying, "You can have them back, I just wanted to prove that I could take them from you," or "I didn't really want them, I just wanted to hurt you like you hurt me." Of course the children suffer the most from this manipulative disruption of their lives. At best it leaves them confused about the value systems of their adult models.

If you feel that your ex is using custody as an excuse to get even with you, do mention it to your lawyer. Most judges do not take kindly to parents using the children against each other, and if your attorney can find a way to prove this in court it can be a point in your favor. It's a hard one to prove, however, and if other factors weigh heavily against you, it probably won't matter at all.

Your home environment is going to be taken strongly into account so if there is anything unusual or "abnormal" about your household, be sure to mention it to your lawyer. Expect at least one and possibly many visits from social workers and other representatives of child welfare agencies. They will be examining the environment in which you propose to raise your kids. Ideally they will be neutral with respect to your sexual orientation, but don't count on it. Although social workers are supposedly up to date on information about homosexuality and how it relates to stability and nurturing, many of them hold their own prejudices and opinions about what is a "healthy" environment for kids. More than one case has been lost because of a caseworker's report that read something like: "Parent is a loving, committed parent who provides a warm and supportive environment. *However* . . . . in light of parent's admitted sexual orientation, I do not think that it is in the children's best interest to remain in a situation where they are exposed to questionable influences." What those unsavory influences are or how they are determined is not always clear. More often it appears to reflect the caseworker's personal prejudice about homosexuality and the lack of knowledge of the research done on gay parenting. If you feel that the observer assigned to check out your home environment was prejudiced, about the most you can realistically do is try to have more than one social worker visit your home.

If it sounds as if I'm telling you to expect homophobic reactions around every corner, you're probably right. The bulk of information regarding custody cases shows that most people involved in the decision-making process are not familiar enough with homosexual issues and psychology to make an unbiased appraisal. The best you can hope for is an assessment by someone who considers homosexuality irrelevant to good parenting.

The question of relevance is an important one, particularly at the outset of your case. Most of the lawyers experienced in gay and lesbian custody disputes agree that trying to hide a parent's sexual orientation is unwise unless other factors are so overwhelming that a case for good parenting could not otherwise be made. Unless you choose to remain celibate and isolated from the rest of the gay community until your child reaches majority, trying to hide your homosexuality isn't likely to work. If your ex-spouse knows about your orientation, it is practically useless.

It is important to realize that *a custody decision is never final.* Many parents assume that once they have custody, they will retain custody until their child becomes an adult. This is simply not so. Your ex or even a relative can reopen the dispute at any time claiming that a "change in circumstances" warrants removing the child from your care. In many states, discovery that a parent is gay is viewed as a sufficient "change in circumstances." Essentially, this means that hiding it in the initial custody hearing is a limited move. If you hide it then, you must continue to hide it or the whole process can start all over again. If a parent or relative sues for removal of the child on grounds that you hid your homosexuality the first time around, the burden of proof is going to fall on you to prove that it doesn't matter. This isn't the way the law reads; technically, they must prove that it *does* matter. Practically, however, parents who go back to court because of newly disclosed information generally end up having to defend themselves against negative allegations. The fact that you "covered up" something the first time around doesn't look good in court.

Because hiding your orientation is so chancy, most attorneys will attempt to have it ruled irrelevant early on in the proceedings. If they succeed, the parent's sexual orientation will be known and on record but may not (ostensibly) be used in making the final determination of who will get custody. It doesn't always work and it doesn't mean that a homophobic judge won't take it into consideration anyway, but it eliminates much of the harassment and mudslinging that can go on when homosexuality is the primary issue under consideration. It also means that if the judgment goes against you and your sexual orientation appears to be reflected in that judgment, you may have grounds to appeal to a higher court.

The attempt to get your sexuality ruled irrelevant also gives your lawyer an opportunity to educate the judge. Even if it is allowed as an issue, the lawyer's initial request for such a ruling can include material to substantiate the position (e.g., studies that show that there is very little difference between lesbian and straight mothers, papers attesting to the stability of homosexuals in general, etc.). Such material provided in the early stages, however, should never take the place of expert testimony later on. Never assume that the judge has read all the paperwork before coming to court. He probably has, but it's not a chance you want to take.

Assuming that your sexual orientation is allowed as an issue in the trial, one thing you are going to need is *expert testimony.* This can include testimony from psychology and child-development professionals. Experts called in to testify should be familiar with and experienced in situations such as yours. Preferably a psychiatrist or psychologist should have worked with both straight and gay parents and know the research done in these areas. They should have met you, your child or children and, if possible, your ex-partner, and they should be prepared to give a professional assessment. You may also want to have an expert witness available to answer questions about homosexuality in general. A professional is much better equipped to deal with ignorance and prurient questions such as "What do lesbians do together?" Your expert should have respectable credentials and a trustworthy manner. It has also been recommended that the expert witness be coached by the lawyer in presentation and appearance. It should not matter whether your expert is straight or gay, but many lawyers prefer a heterosexual witness because the court is likely to perceive him or her as less biased. In any case, your attorney should select the witness carefully. An expert without practical experience or (prejudice again) sporting shoulder-length hair or outrageous clothing could do more harm than good. (Don't laugh; an experienced attorney speaks ruefully of the expert witness she neglected to coach on his appearance who turned up in court with a silver suit and gaudy jewelry, ruining his professional credibility with the court.)

Expect to be examined by an expert witness (most likely a psychiatrist or psychologist) retained by the other party. It will be this person's job to look for psychological traits that render you an unfit parent. Be cooperative but cautious when dealing with such people. A psychologist retained by you may be helpful in preparing you for such an interview.

In addition to expert witnesses, your lawyer may want to call some *character witnesses* to testify on your behalf. These can include neighbors, church members, children's teachers and various other people who have known you and your children and are willing to testify to your positive qualities as a parent. Generally, the more "normal" (i.e., heterosexual, middle-class, stable) they are the better, and if they are parents themselves or have a particularly traditional role, so much the better. If these people are reluctant to present themselves in court, notarized letters of recommendation may also be useful and easier to obtain.

Your lawyer will want to make very sure that your character witnesses' testimony will hold up under cross-examination. Do not recommend anyone as a witness unless you feel confident of his or her goodwill and presentability.

Lovers

If you have a lover at the time of the hearing, particularly if you live together, it is likely that he or she will be asked to testify. Don't underestimate the strain this can put on your relationship. It's a very difficult position for a lover to be put in; the fear is always there that something she or he will say will make a crucial difference. Also, your lover may not be as willing as you are to adjust his or her dress and life-style for the sake of a custody battle. This is something you will need to discuss thoroughly together. It is unfair to expect your partner to make radical changes to accommodate you. On the other hand, it is unfair to yourself to try to divide your loyalties at such a crucial time. In the case of many divorcing parents who are just coming out, the gay relationship itself is very new. The strain of developing a positive bond in the midst of the upheaval surrounding custody may be more than either of you can handle. Some men and women have found that counseling is helpful at this time for both parent and lover. Therapists who specialize in gay couple counseling should be considered. Such a therapist may give you both the sounding board you need and take some of the stress off your time together.

The courts have often passed rulings on gay parent custody that reflected a parent's involvement with a lover. Ignorance and prejudice have resulted in a number of cases where the parent's custody or visitation is contingent upon the lover's living separately or never seeing the parent when the children are present.

Many of the parents in our survey indicated that they were particularly cautious about expressing physical affection toward their lovers while their children were in the room. This self-imposed limitation sometimes went as far as kissing or handholding —certainly not perceived as lewd behavior when performed by heterosexuals. Yet it seems that some judges would rather a child witnessed a heterosexual orgy than a gay couple holding hands and watching television.

Because of the precedents set in earlier cases, you and your lover may be counseled to live apart until the case is settled. You will have to discuss this carefully with your lover.

On the brighter side, some judges have chosen to look at the gay or lesbian family as simply an alternative family unit. Recent research conducted at Stanford University has shown that children appear to do better (i.e., less delinquency, better school performance, etc.) when there is more than one adult present in the household to provide supervision. The sexes or relationships of the adults are less significant than the guidance they give and the stability they provide. More enlightened courts will take into account the benefits of two-adult households and we can hope that, in the future, having a lover will be an asset to a gay parent seeking custody.

However you choose to approach custody as a gay parent with a lover, you will need to be prepared for stress. Communication, mutual support and other interests for both of you will help keep the relationship intact. You will need to reach an agreement on crucial issues of life-style and environment and you must let your lawyer know that you have a steady relationship.

Continuity

One of the criteria to which you can expect the judge to give great weight is where your child has been living up to the time of the hearing. Stability and continuity of environment are considered to be in the best interests of the child and most judges are reluctant to upset a stable household unless they are sure that other conditions render it necessary. The longer your child has lived with you prior to the hearing, the better chance you have of convincing the judge that the child should remain there.

Lawyers experienced in custody cases will strongly urge you to live with your child prior to the hearing if it is at all possible. If not, visit as frequently as you can. In an adversary court situation you will need to prove your consistent effort to provide steady, long-term support to your child or children. Although you may feel a need for "time off" or a breathing spell after divorce, resist the urge to leave the child in your ex-partner's care for "a little while" if you sincerely want to seek permanent custody. Of course, this is not to advocate battles that may be traumatic to the children. Nor are we recommending that you kidnap a child from your ex.

A word or two here on "kidnapping." Removing a child from his or her customary home without the consent or knowledge of the supervising adult is a serious crime in most states. Taking a child over state lines complicates this still further and the end result may very well be criminal prosecution and complete loss of custody. If you feel that your child is in danger of physical or psychological harm from your ex-partner, try to gather evidence to this end so that you can approach it in a legally appropriate way. If you do not think you stand any chance of gaining custody regardless of your ex's instability, consider trying to have the child put in the custody of a third party—a grandparent or other stable adult. You may not be any closer to having custody yourself but you will have peace of mind knowing that your child is safe.

The Sex of the Parent

It would be misleading to present material on custody issues without a realistic examination of the effect a parent's sex has on the outcome. The legal system is usually slow to catch up with social trends; it is a bastion of traditional thinking and must be approached accordingly. Therefore, whatever one's views on sex roles and parenting, the fact is that female parents are usually given priority over male parents, particularly when the male parent is a homosexual.

That lesbian mothers face a struggle in gaining custody is undeniable. But they have one thing going for them that gay fathers do not: they are mothers and (for the last hundred years anyway) social and legal preference has been for mothers to raise children after a divorce. Even those of us who consciously examine gender roles often defer to the role of mother, assuming that, by the very nature of her sex, she is the more involved parent. Social conditioning of fathers has reinforced this belief, discouraging them from close, intimate bonding with their children, and instead judging their parenting ability by their skills as providers. A man's nurturing role is downplayed or discouraged. Many men today—both gay and straight—are challenging these notions. They are claiming their right to be involved with children on a warm, interpersonal level and rejecting the archetype of "father" as the stern, distant breadwinner. The transition, however, is just beginning and the committed father facing today's legal systems is up against many obstacles.

Gay fathers face a double prejudice in court: their affectional orientation and their sex. Even if they do manage to convince a judge that homosexuality has no bearing on parenting ability, they may be hard pressed to win the argument that they are the better parents—particularly when all other things appear equal.

Over half the fathers who completed preliminary questionnaires had custody of their children. I found this encouraging, yet, when they were questioned further, a trend emerged that was different from the one I had initially expected. Most of the custodial fathers had not gone through the court system. They had gained custody either because of a cooperative spouse (more common for gay men than for lesbian women), a negligent spouse (in which case custody was essentially by default), adoption or the death of the marriage partner. A few had custody based on an older child's choice. The fathers who had won custody in court—on an even footing with their ex-spouses—were a tiny minority. By far most of the noncustodial fathers had not even tried to gain custody. This is not to say that they did not want custody; many of them did. But time and again they had been advised that theirs was a losing battle. Or they had decided that the risk of coming out was too great or that the children would "of course" be better off with their mothers.

These were not weak or apolitical men. Many of them had agonized over the loss of contact with children with whom they had had close, nurturing relationships up to the time of divorce. However, they were caught in between the changing roles society assigns men: encouraged by the feminist and gay liberation ideologies to be involved, nurturing parents but denied equal consideration in court because of traditional assumptions about parenting roles. Whether they won or lost, we need to applaud the men who had the courage to challenge those assumptions and seek custody when they felt it was in the children's best interests.

Custody Granted to a Third Party

This is something many parents (on both sides of the gay issue) have probably never considered. In a really bitter custody dispute, with both sides doing a good job of proving the other incompetent, the court does not have to grant custody to either parent. A judge, after hearing everyone's arguments, may decide that neither of you is a fit parent and either make the children wards of the court or remand them into the custody of a relative. This is a fairly rare occurrence, but it has happened. Third-party custody is a potential byproduct of the adversary system set up to determine custody disputes. When both you and your ex-spouse are put in the position of discrediting each other, it's possible to do too good a job. Some lawyers, realizing this, will concentrate on proving why their client *should* have custody rather than dwelling on why the other parent should not.

In other third-party custody disputes involving homosexual parents, a relative has initiated the suit, attempting to gain custody of a minor child on the grounds that the custodial parent's gayness is detrimental to the children. One woman had the devastating experience of her own parents going to court to get custody of her son after they discovered that she was a lesbian. As with ex-spouse situations, the court will look at where the child has been living all along and how well-adjusted the child is. If you have had custody of your child for a long period of time, a relative's chances of gaining custody are greatly reduced.

There are a few instances in which some other, unrelated party has actively sought to remove a child from the custody of a lesbian or gay parent. Such interference is rare when the child is well-adjusted and the home is warm and supportive. Usually action of this type is generated by complaints of neglect from child welfare agencies or a history of delinquency on the part of the child or children. Most state agencies have far too big a backlog of real problems to challenge a stable home. You should, however, be aware that, in some localities, being gay is enough to generate complaints against you as a parent. Most state-funded welfare agencies are required to check into such complaints. If you find your suitability as a parent in question by child-welfare officials, I urge you to hire a lawyer. A majority of such unprovoked investigations blow over but it is better to be prepared than sorry.

Hope for the Future

If, after all of these cautions and conditions, you do decide to weather the storms of a custody dispute, take heart. As more and more people in our culture are educated about the realities of homosexuality, the chances for you and your children to lead a normal life together increase. There are judges out there who will give you that chance, just as there are those who will oppose you. Ten years ago, by one lawyer's estimate, you had no better than a 10 percent chance of gaining custody if homosexuality was the main issue. Today, in some areas of the country, you have an even chance. Some judges are looking at you as a parent, not as a homosexual. Some of them even have a sense of humor about it: one judge went on record as saying that he didn't care if the mother's love object was a sewing machine as long as she was a good parent. And there are a few courts in this land of ours who recognize that human dignity and love are truly the most important qualities of all.

Perhaps the most eloquent illustration of that understanding was shown in 1979 by Judge Antell of New Jersey, who stated in response to the idea that a plaintiff's children might be embarrassed by her lesbianism:

> If defendant retains custody, it may be that because the community is intolerant of her differences, these girls may sometimes have to bear themselves with greater than ordinary fortitude. But this does not necessarily portend that their moral welfare or safety will be jeopardized. It is just as reasonable to expect that they will emerge better equipped to search out their own standards of right and wrong, better able to perceive that the majority is not always correct in its moral judgements, and better able to understand the importance of conforming their beliefs to the requirements of reason and tested knowledge, not the constraints of currently popular sentiment or prejudice. Taking the children from the defendant can be done only at the cost of sacrificing those very qualities they will find most sustaining in meeting the challenges inevitably ahead.

Instead of forbearance and feelings of protectiveness, it will foster in them a sense of shame for their mother. Instead of courage and the precept that people of integrity do not shrink from bigots, it counsels the easy option of shirking difficult problems and following the course of expedience. Lastly, it diminishes their regard for the rule of human behavior . . . that we do not forsake those to whom we are indebted for love and nurturing merely because they are held in low esteem by others.

Judge Antell concludes,

extensive evidence in the record . . . amply confirms the trial judge's finding that the defendant is a worthy mother. Nothing suggests that her homosexual preference in itself presents any threat of harm to her daughters or that in the ordinary course of their development they will be unable to deal with whatever vexation may be caused to their spirits by the community.

VISITATION

If you lose custody of your children in court, you should be prepared to discuss your visitation rights. If you choose not to be a custodial parent (whether because you expect to lose in court or out of personal preference), you will still need to establish the boundaries of visitation rights at the time of divorce. Most states grant visitation to noncustodial parents as a matter of course unless it is established that such visitation will be detrimental to the child. The extent of those rights remains to be negotiated and agreed upon by both parents.

As a gay or lesbian parent you will probably find that extensive visitation is much easier to gain than full legal custody. This does *not,* however, mean that you can *expect* it to be uncontested if you and your former spouse are on bad terms. A hostile ex can attempt to block visitation by assserting that *any* exposure to you would be detrimental to the children. Using the same arguments that arise in a custody struggle, your ex-spouse may try to convince the judge that you are dangerous, an immoral influence, irresponsible about the children's welfare, or all of the above and more. Though the precedent is less severe in visitation negotiations, the lesbian or gay parent divorcing under strained circumstances must be prepared to deal with these issues should they arise.

Many of the arguments concerning custody apply to visitation as well. In the determination of visitation rights, however, extra emphasis will be placed on your appearance, your reliability and the company you keep. If your visitation includes the right to keep the children overnight, the condition of your home and the presence of lovers and roommates need to be considered. Some courts have been known to grant visitation subject to very specific limitations (e.g., that the gay parent's lover not be present, that visitation take place only in the home of the ex-spouse or some other relative or that the visiting parent not keep the children overnight). Before you appear in court, you and your attorney should have worked out just what amount of visitation you want and how far you are willing to go to obtain those rights.

As with custody, it will help you and save court costs if you and your former partner can reach an agreeable arrangement between yourselves. You may discover that your ex-spouse is much more open to extensive visitation than you expected. It is important that you discuss the issue with her or him. If you can negotiate an acceptable arrangement and have it ready to present the judge, a struggle can potentially be avoided or defused. The judge does not have to go along with your agreement but the odds are good that he or she will unless you have a very unusual arrangement. Most judges see themselves as being available to settle disagreements and are not anxious to interfere with an agreement that seems reasonable and legal.

There are many reasons for parents to choose visitation over custody. Some see it as a rational means to avoid the mess and upset of a legal fight and have been quite satisfied. Some are eager to live alone and explore the world for the first time and find that extensive visitation is exactly what they want. For many, it is a bitter second best. Some of the people we talked to wound up with extremely limited visitation because they had concentrated so hard on winning custody that they never planned for the possibility of visitation and were unprepared to negotiate fair terms.

Linda, a lesbian of about thirty-five, told me that she had something she wanted to get off her chest, even though I "probably wouldn't be able to use it, being so proparenting."

"I don't really like kids," she told me in a low voice. "I have two and they're okay, I guess, but I never wanted children and I don't particularly enjoy being around them. I gave their dad custody when we divorced and I'm glad I did!"

Men and women like Linda should be commended rather than censured for their honesty. By choosing visitation (to whatever degree) over socially obligated custody, they probably do more good for their children than if they had fought. Not everyone is cut out to be a parent. When making a choice between custody and visitation, it is important to be honest with yourself. Choosing to fight for custody out of guilt or conditioning may not be in the best interests of your children. It's not fair to a young person to have to bear the brunt of an unwilling parent's resentment.

Typically, visitation is granted a noncustodial parent in order to ensure maximum contact with both parents. The court will try to keep in mind the child's needs, schedules and stability. You may be granted the right to visit your child during particular evenings, on weekends (every weekend, once a month, twice a month, etc.) and for part of some or all school vacations. There is often a set schedule and you may be required to notify the custodial parent in advance of any and all visits so that schedules can be coordinated appropriately. If your ex-spouse is cooperative and your parting amicable, you may find yourself spending almost as much time with your kids as you did when you lived together. Some parents report that they spend *more* time in direct interaction with their children than they did during the marriage or that the time spent together is of a better quality because it is more conscious.

Lesbian and gay parents who did not have custody of their children were frequently perplexed by the challenge of integrating their social lives with weekend visitation. Though the children came first, more than once I heard the lament, "I never meet anyone because I spend all my free time with my kids!" You are going to have to decide how your personal schedule and your social life interact with those of your children. In cases where the court has been prone to award noncustodial parents visitation on alternate weekends, some parents have negotiated for the option of seeing the children *every* Friday night or Sunday afternoon, thus keeping a day open for adult social activities. Others scheme to find events which both they and their children can enjoy, such as picnics, softball games, parades. After a year or two of weekend visits, new activities are hard to find and a lot of people settle into a routine of quiet Sunday afternoons at home or at Grandma's house. They are often surprised to find that the parent-child relationship improves at this point as communication takes priority over entertainment.

It seems appropriate here to bring up an often neglected point about visitation. In the last few years a movement has arisen designed to give grandparents visitation rights after divorce. In the struggle of two parents to separate their lives and property and to establish a stable environment for the children, the feelings and needs of the divorcing couple's families may be overlooked. It can be a bitter blow to both grandparent and child if the effect of divorce is separation from a beloved relative. The wise parent is aware of this and will make some efforts to nurture family bonds. While it is still considered unorthodox, you may want to consider visitation for grandparents as part of your negotiations. This might be (with the grandparents' agreement) the establishing of regular visits, Christmas dinners or simply the right for your child to talk to his or her grandparents on the telephone once a month. This can be particularly valuable if you should die or if difficulties arise between you and your ex at some future time.

GUARDIANSHIPS

There have been a few situations where a lesbian or gay individual was given legal custody of a minor child even though they were not biologically related. I think that these people amply qualify as gay parents. It is the relationship, not the genealogy of those involved, that counts.

In 1977 a Denver, Colorado, court awarded custody of a seven-year-old girl to her deceased mother's former lover, a woman who had developed a strong, nurturing and parental relationship with the child. In this unique case, the court was able to rise above bias and consider primarily the woman's parenting abilities and the child's welfare.

In his decision, the judge stated:

> Donna's sexual preference has not affected the child in the past and is not related to her ability to parent the child. Her strengths as a parent . . . are her sensitivity, her ability to empathize . . . , her warmth and her dependability. When sexual preference would become significant . . . Donna has the ability to deal with it intelligently, openly, and honestly. She prefers that the child have what is considered by society as a normal life of boyfriends, dating and marriage, and later on children.

It is gratifying to know that such judges exist, though it would be foolish to expect this sort of understanding in most courtrooms today. Clearly the woman's past experience in raising the youngster and the child's healthy development were instrumental in gaining this custody award. One wonders, however, what the outcome would have been if Donna hadn't expressed a preference that the child have "what is considered by society as a normal life"?

A woman from Ohio was granted custody of her dependent niece. Other family members had fought this decision but the woman's history of stability, her strong religious and community values and her occupation as a schoolteacher convinced the courts that she was the best "parent" for the girl, her lesbianism not withstanding. This remarkable woman emphasized the importance of community involvement and support from her fellow church members in winning her fight for custody; she urged that others who seek custody of children not their own establish themselves strongly in the traditional community so that the gay issue becomes a minor point in establishing fitness to parent.

Her advice appears well grounded, though there is too little data available on nonbiological relatives' gaining custody to formulate anything resembling practical guidelines. Those individuals who have been given custody or appointed guardians all had a strong, parental relationship with the child prior to going to court. They went in with the precedent of nurturing ability held up for the judge to see. Both of the women discussed above appeared to be stable financially and psychologically, presenting themselves well in the courtroom. One man who had guardianship of someone else's children was less conventional: he had moved several times across the United States, held odd jobs, lived in the woods without amenities. His guardianship was of children he considered stepchildren, having been born to a woman to whom he was, at one time, married. She voluntarily appointed him the children's legal guardian. There was no official custody hearing; rather, personal agreement and expedience led to the arrangement.

The gay man or lesbian who wishes to appoint a gay friend or lover guardian to his or her children in the event of the parent's death should consult a competent attorney familiar with gay issues. It will need to be explicitly and emphatically stated in the parent's will so that the court is aware of the parent's wishes. Even so, the appointed guardian may face a powerful challenge, particularly if there are close living relatives. In most states, the appointed guardian is subject to approval by the juvenile courts; the parent's will is not the final authority. The courts will go along with the deceased's wishes if they deem them suitable and if no one contests them, but the guardian may find himself or herself in court fighting against the child's grandparents or other blood relatives. Whenever possible, judges like to place the children of deceased parents with members of the family. It is going to be up to your appointed guardian to prove that he or she is a closer member of the child's family than anyone else.

The more involved the appointed guardian has been in the child's upbringing, the more favorable are the chances for successful litigation. If your chosen guardian is a lover who has lived with you and your children and participated in their care, he or she is more likely to be looked upon as a parental figure. Acceptance of this individual as a parent on the part of your family may also be helpful. If they are accustomed to seeing your friend or partner in a warm, nurturing light, they will be less inclined to fight for custody in the event of your death. One attorney I spoke with suggested obtaining a signed, notarized statement from members of your immediate family (specifically parents, brothers and sisters —relations most likely to be considered for guardianship) stating clearly that they acknowledge and accept your partner as the child's legal guardian in the event of your death. This could carry much weight, but it may be a difficult document to obtain, even if your family appears accepting. It's worth a try, though.

TWELVE

Supplemental Nurturing

The world would be a very different place if everyone had unlimited energy and enthusiasm to give to the next generation. In reality, there are a lot of people out there who genuinely love kids, understand them and have things to teach, but who simply don't have the resources or interest to be full-time parents.

Sheila lives on a small farm in Oregon with her son Denny, who is two. They live in relative isolation, eking out a bare but satisfying living from the earth and Sheila's pottery skills. Their nearest neighbor is almost a mile away; they get into the small town nearby a few times a month. When Denny is old enough for school, he will travel by bus almost twenty miles each way. This way of life is exactly what Sheila wants, precisely how she planned her future with her child—peace, quiet and self-reliance.

Denny's father, Robert, lives in Seattle, many hours' drive from his son's rural home. Every second weekend he drives down to

Oregon to spend a day or two with Sheila and Denny. During his two-week vacation each summer he takes Denny to Minnesota to visit his grandparents while Sheila attends a women's music festival. He is an enthusiastic parent who admits to "spoiling my kid a little because I don't see him a lot. I don't have to do the disciplining." Being a parent fifty-odd days a year suits him just fine. So far the arrangement between himself and Sheila has been working very well.

Initially, Sheila had considered artificial insemination with an unknown donor. She had no desire to share her quiet life-style with another adult, though she was very certain that she wanted a child. But, after talking to a number of women who had conceived by unknown-donor insemination, she decided, "It would be nice to have someone else in the picture—just a little bit. Somebody else who would be interested in Denny's development, who could give him some diversity in his little life. And I thought it would be nice if he knew his father. If it were me, I'd sure want to know when I grew up who he was, what he did, where he lived. But I didn't want someone in my life all the time—not somebody close by who would just drop in unannounced. So I started looking at men I know who lived far away."

She had known Robert from craft fairs where they displayed their work, and had seen how well he related to the children who came to the fairs. He was something of a Pied Piper with kids—warm, funny, full of stories. And he lived more than seven hundred miles away. Carefully she broached the subject to him. His enthusiasm was immediate: he confessed that he had investigated Big Brother programs in his hometown and was saddened to be told that his obvious homosexuality made him (in their opinion) unsuitable. When Sheila suggested that he become a supplemental parent, helping to conceive and then visiting on occasion, he mulled the idea over for a few days and agreed. More out of curiosity than anything else, they decided to attempt conception through intercourse. To their surprise (and amusement), Sheila got pregnant on the first try.

"It made us more relaxed with each other," Robert admits, grinning. "Although, in retrospect, it could've been a disaster, if it hadn't worked. But it did. Sex with Sheila didn't make me convert to straight sex or anything, but it let me know that it's not such a big deal. It was nice to know that I was there when it happened, not at the other end of a test tube or something."

Randy, on the other hand, considers himself a supplemental parent to three-year-old Debbie even though he is not her biological father and had nothing to do with her conception and birth. Her mother, Karen, is a single heterosexual woman who loves children but wondered if she was up to coping with the stresses of single parenthood. When she discovered she was pregnant by a former lover, she went through a serious moral debate about whether or not to keep the child, soliciting advice from friends of every possible perspective.

"I need time to myself," she stated very directly. "Not every day, but certainly every week. I didn't think it would be fair to a baby to have this screaming lunatic for a mother if I couldn't occasionally have some time off to just be alone." Enter Randy, a coworker and father to two boys who live across the country. He has not seen his sons in several years.

"From the start, I offered to play father surrogate whenever it got to be too much for Karen. I miss my own kids tremendously. I was a really involved parent when they were babies so the diapers, burping and 2 A.M. feedings were no surprise. I'm against abortions for the most part; I do think there are exceptions but as a general birth-control method I'm opposed. So when she said she was considering one, I really gave her a pitch. I even considered adopting the baby myself. But in the end she decided she did want to be a mother—as long as she had some help."

Randy works for an airline and his hours are erratic. A regular routine of joint care would be out of the question, according to them both. But for a day or two each week, Debbie lives in Randy's apartment and calls him "Daddy." She came up with the title herself without encouragement and much to everyone's surprise. And he is a daddy, sharing, loving, bathing and cuddling the little girl he has cared for since birth.

"I've got a college fund started for her," he acknowledged. "It's a lifetime commitment."

Is supplemental parenting a sort of big-brother or big-sister program with long-term contracts? In many respects it certainly is. And yet it often goes far beyond simple volunteerism. Even a day a month creates over the course of years a tremendous bond between adult and child.

Most often it appears that men are the supplemental parents, biological or not. But increasingly women are choosing to become involved with someone else's child rather than having one of their own. For the most part they are intelligent, well-organized people who simply recognize that their priorities don't include full-time parenthood. As one woman said, "It wouldn't be fair—to me or the kid. I'm committed to so many things that I haven't time to devote my life to a little one. It's better as it is, helping Annie raise her son a day or so a week. We all benefit. She gets time off, he gets a change of pace and me, I just do what I can."

As the parenting network expands, a wide variety of people are discovering that the presence of children can be an asset—not only to those of us who choose to conceive or adopt and commit a major part of our lives, but to our friends as well. Being a big friend to a little person gives outlet to creative energies, nurturing abilities and the need to play that so many adults stifle. We need not choose full-time parenting to be involved with kids, any more than we must give up the option of parenting because we are gay. There is room for many levels of healthy, nurturing involvement between children and adults, all of which ultimately benefit the kids.

Within the gay and lesbian communities of North America, we have created a multilayered and many-faceted society, capable of encompassing a wide spectrum of life-styles. As we expand these communities, we are finding both room and need to share this rich, varied world with children—our own and others'. Throughout history, gay men and lesbians have been innovators, creative spirits and heralds of social change. As we seek to expand our horizons and invest our nurturing energy in another generation of human beings, let's hope that we can pass on to them our best selves—generous, talented and possessing a tremendous capacity for love.

APPENDIX ONE

Resource Guide to Services and Organizations

PARENT GROUPS

PARENTS SUPPORT GROUP, PHOENIX, Box 32441, Phoenix, AZ 85064

GAY PARENTS GROUP, c/o GLAD, Box 117, Tempe, AZ 85281

LESBIAN/GAY PARENTING RAP, c/o Diablo Valley Community Center, 1818 Colfax Avenue, Concord, CA 94520

GAY AND LESBIAN PARENTING GROUP, Berkeley, CA, Ron (415) 841-4622

PARENTS GROUP, c/o Gay Community Service Center, Box 36777, Los Angeles, CA 90038, (213) 464-7400

GAY MOTHERS AND FATHERS, SAN DIEGO, c/o Gay Community Center, 1447 30th Street, San Diego, CA 92102

GAY MOTHERS AND GAY FATHERS, c/o The Gay Center, 2250 B Street, San Diego, CA 92102, (714) 232-7528

LESBIAN AND GAY COPARENTING GROUP, 806 Haight Street, San Francisco, CA 94117, (415) 863-9413

GAY PARENTS GROUP, 2131 Union Street, San Francisco, CA 94123

PARENTS LOVERS AND CHILDREN'S GROUP, San Francisco, CA, (415) 751-1977

GAY FATHERS AND LESBIAN MOTHERS, c/o GATE, Box 1852, Edmonton, Alberta, CN T5J 2P2

GAY PARENTS, c/o Gays for Equality, Box 27, UMSU, University of Manitoba, Winnipeg, Manitoba, CN R3T 2N2, (204) 269-8678

GAY PARENTS ASSOCIATION, c/o Gay/Lesbian Community Center, 1436 Lafayette Street, Denver, CO 80218

LESBIAN MOTHERS AND GAY FATHERS, Washington, DC, (202) 548-3238

GAY PARENTS SUPPORT GROUP, c/o Center for Dialogue, 2175 Northwest 26th Street, Miami, FL 33142

SEXUAL IDENTITY CENTER, Box 3244, 2139 Kuhio Avenue, Honolulu, HI 96801, (808) 926-1000. *Has sponsored support groups for parents. Group for relatives of gays. Call or write.*

PARENTS GROUP, c/o Gay Horizons Center, 3225 North Sheffield Avenue, Chicago, IL 60657, (312) 929-HELP

GAY PARENTS ASSOCIATION, c/o M. Connell, 930 North Broadway, No. B, Wichita, KS 67214

GAY PARENTS GROUP, c/o Steve Clemmenth, 3907 East Mount Vernon Street, Wichita, KS 67218

GAY PARENTS SUPPORT GROUP, c/o St. Louis Community Center, 1022 Barracks Street, New Orleans, LA 70116

PARENTS WHO ARE GAY, P.O. Box 548, Columbia, MD 21045. *Fathers—c/o Billy (301) 997-3541. Mothers—c/o Darlene (301) 568-6532.*

LESBIAN MOTHERS/GAY FATHERS, P.O. Box 25, Laurel, MD 20810

GAY/LESBIAN PARENTS OF PORTLAND, c/o F. Brooks, 26 Cushman Street, Portland, ME 04102

GAY PARENTS, 348 West 14th Street, New York, NY 10014, (212) 242-6616

PARENTS GROUP, c/o Dayton Gay Center, 665 Salem Avenue, Dayton, OH 45405, (614) 228-4875

GAY PARENTS, DALLAS, 3444 Normandy Street, Dallas, TX 75205, (214) 528-1024

GAY PARENTS GROUP, c/o AURA, P.O. Box 7318, Fort Worth, TX 76111

GAY AND LESBIAN PARENTS SUPPORT GROUP, Montrose Counseling Center, 900 Lovett, No. 203, Houston, TX 77006

GAY PARENTS GROUP, P.O. Box 1170, Seattle, WA 98111

COUNSELING

PACIFIC CENTER FOR HUMAN GROWTH, 2712 Telegraph Avenue, Berkeley, CA 94704. *They have rap groups for gays and lesbians of all ages.*

OPEN QUEST INSTITUTE, 3808 Udell Court, Los Angeles, CA 90027

FAE PANNER, L.A. Women's Therapy Center, 12581 Venice Boulevard, Los Angeles, CA 90066

MARGERY SHELTON, M.S.W., 1401 Sanborn Avenue, Los Angeles, CA

DAVID L. LUNDQUIST, L.C.S.W., 683 North Calle Marcus, Palm Springs, CA 92262, (619) 323-8025. *Specialist in child psychotherapy and legal issues.*

GEORGE DEABILL, M.S., Box 11363A, Palo Alto, CA 94306

TIMOTHY WOLF, 2423 Camino del Rio South, No. 111, San Diego, CA 92108

OPERATION CONCERN, Box 7999, San Francisco, CA 94120, (526) 563-0202. *Professional counseling for gay people and their families.*

GAY COUNSELING GROUP, The Bridge, 640 Campus Drive, Stanford, CA 94305, (415) 497-3392. *Mon.–Fri. 4–7 p.m. Ask for gay counselor.*

BRIAN MILLER, M.F.C.C., Ph.D., 8235 Santa Monica Boulevard, No. 307, West Hollywood, CA 90046, (213) 660-4495. *Extensive experience with gay married men. Published papers on subject of gay fathers.*

GAY HORIZONS COMMUNITY CENTER, 3225 North Sheffield Avenue, Chicago, IL 60657, (312) 929-HELP. *Provides resources. Has sponsored parents groups. Hotline, call 929-HELP.*

ANDREW MATTISON, Psychologist, 814 Blackhawk Drive, Park Forest, IL 60466, (312) 534-2470. *Specialist in gay men and women. Has done important research with married gays.*

GAY AND LESBIAN COUNSELING SERVICE, 80 Boylston Street, No. 855, Boston, MA 02116, (617) 542-5188. *Licensed mental health clinic serving the gay community—educational to mental health.*

MIRIAM ROSENBERG, M.D., Ph.D., Boston, MA, (617) 358-7512. *Psychiatrist specializing in lesbian and gay adolescents, children of gays and lesbian custody.*

JOSEPH LAMOTT, 24 Elm Street, No. 10, Westfield, MA 01086

LESBIAN AND GAY COMMUNITY SERVICES, 124 West Lake Street, Minneapolis, MN 55408, (612) 827-2821. *Mental health clinic.*

TOD BERGMAN, M.S.W., 324 Garden Street, Hoboken, NJ 07030, (201) 798-8289. *Special sensitivity to gay parents. NYC office: (212) 255-3566.*

NATIONAL ASSOCIATION OF SOCIAL WORKERS TASK FORCE ON GAY AND LESBIAN ISSUES, 110 West State Street, Trenton, NJ 08608, (609) 394-1666. *Resource list of therapists for lesbian and gay clients. Bibliography, speakers bureau.*

PEER COUNSEL, Box 812, Santa Fe, NM 87501, (505) 983-5598. *By appointment; twenty-four-hour phone; counseling and referral at no charge.*

E. SUE BLUME, C.S.W., Hempstead, Long Island, NY, (516) 483-7883. *Counseling for parents of lesbians and gays.*

CHARLES PUGLISI, Ph.D., Box 161, Middle Valley, NY 11379

ASSOCIATION OF GAY PSYCHOLOGISTS, 210 Fifth Avenue, New York, NY 10010

GLORIA BACK, M.S.W., C.S.W., 135 East 83rd Street, No. 4D, New York, NY 10028, (212) 861-6998. *Practice of social work limited to families of gay people.*

GOTHAM PSYCHOTHERAPY ASSOCIATES, New York, NY, (212) 903-4033. *By appointment; specializing in lesbian and gay life-styles.*

ROBERT GOULD, M.D., 144 East End Avenue, New York, NY 10028, (212) 535-7275. *Psychiatrist; can provide expert testimony.*

HOMOSEXUAL COMMUNITY COUNSELING CENTER, 30 East 60th Street, New York, NY 10022, (212) 688-0628. *By appointment.*

IDENTITY HOUSE, 544 Sixth Avenue, New York, NY 10011, (212) 243-8181. *Free walk-in peer counseling, rap groups, therapy, referrals.*

INSTITUTE FOR HUMAN IDENTITY, INC., 490 West End Avenue, New York, NY 10024, (212) 799-9432. *Psychotherapy for gays, rap groups, training program for students in clinical fields.*

AUDREY STEINHORN, 110 West 86th Street, New York, NY 10024, (212) 799-9190. *Therapist, resource person for foster care and adoption.*

RICHARD GREEN, SUNY at Stonybrook, Nicolls Road (HSC Megastructure), Stonybrook, NY 11794, (516) 444-2581. *Extensive studies with children of gays. Expert testimony.*

NATIONAL CAUCUS OF GAY AND LESBIAN COUNSELORS, Box 216, Jenkintown, PA 19046

EROMIN CENTER, 412 South 16th Street, Philadelphia, PA 19146, (215) 732-3212. *Counseling, foster care, training and education.*

PAUL G. POWELL, M.S.W., 1041 South 6th Street, Philadelphia, PA 19147, (215) 334-3343

POSEIDA INSTITUTE COUNSELING CENTER, 1945 Laskin Road, Virginia Beach, VA 23454, (804) 425-0715

PEPPER SCHWARTZ, Department of Sociology DK-40, University of Washington, Seattle, WA 98195, (206) 543-5872. *Expert witness; researcher regarding the rights of lesbian mothers and foster parents.*

SEATTLE COUNSELING SERVICE FOR SEXUAL MINORITIES, 1505 Broadway, Seattle, WA 98122, (206) 329-8737

GAY COUNSELING SERVICES, 3707 West Michigan Avenue, Milwaukee, WI 53208, (414) 342-2729

FATHERS GROUPS

GAY FATHERS, PHOENIX, Box 23004, Phoenix, AZ 85002, (602) 257-0350

GAY DADS, P.O. Box 5323, Berkeley, CA 94705

SOUTH BAY GAY FATHERS, 1266 White Oaks Road, No. 110, Campbell, CA 95008

SACRAMENTO GAY FATHERS, Sacramento, CA, (916) 441-4594

BAY AREA GAY FATHERS, Box 31622, San Francisco, CA 94131. *Outstanding library; list of articles and bibliography available on request. Also sponsors ex-spouse support group.*

GAY FATHERS SUPPORT GROUP, Box 283, San Francisco, CA 94101

GAY FATHERS UNLIMITED, 625 Post Street, San Francisco, CA 94101

GAY FATHERS SUPPORT GROUP, SAN JOSE, San Jose, CA, (408) 998-3034

GAY FATHERS OF SANTA CLARA COUNTY, c/o Richard, Santa Clara, CA, (408) 238-7878

GAY FATHERS, c/o GIRC, Box 1828, Station M, T2P 2LB, Calgary, Alberta, CN, (403) 234-8973

GAY FATHERS OF HAMILTON, Box 44, Station B, Hamilton, Ontario, CN L8I 715, (807) 523-7055

GAY FATHERS OF TORONTO, P.O. Box 187, Station F, Toronto, Ontario, CN M4Y 2L5. *Well grounded; very active. They have written a support booklet for fathers.*

GAY FATHERS SUPPORT GROUP, 435 Roehampton Avenue, Toronto, Ontario, CN M4P 1S3

GAY FATHERS COALITION, Box 50360, Washington, DC 20004, (202) 548-3238

GAY AND MARRIED MEN'S ASSOCIATION (GAMMA), Box 28317, Washington, DC 20005, (202) 548-3238. *Not really a fathers group but many fathers belong and parenting issues are discussed.*

CHICAGO MEN'S GATHERING, Box 11076, Chicago, IL 60611, (312) 649-0730. *Concerns include gay rights and rights of fathers after divorce; support and nurturing.*

GAY FATHERS COALITION, INDIANAPOLIS, (317) 546-9339

FATHERS IN TRANSITION, GCN Box 6, Boston, MA 02111

GAY FATHERS OF GREATER BOSTON, P.O. BOX 1287, Kendall Square, Cambridge, MA 02142

DON MAGER, 8011 St. Paul Street, Detroit, MI 48214, (313) 824-4819

GAY FATHERS COALITION, KANSAS CITY, Kansas City, MO, (816) 931-4470

GAY DADDIES, 11-48 1/2 East 7th Street, No. 2, New York, NY 10003, (212) 431-1913

GAY FATHERS FORUM of GREATER NEW YORK, 223 East 19th Street, No. 3, c/o Stu Gross, New York, NY 10003, (212) 460-9181. *Social and support group. Monthly events.*

GAY FATHERS GROUP, c/o Henry Weiss, 305 East 40th Street, New York, NY 10016, (212) 682-4167

GAY FATHERS INC., 334 West 87th Street, No. 8A, New York, NY 10024, (212) 580-1146

NATIONAL COALITION OF GAY FATHERS, 146 East 30th Street, New York, NY 10016

HUSBANDS/FATHERS OF CENTRAL NEW YORK, Box 6452, Syracuse, NY 13217

GAY FATHERS OF WESTCHESTER, c/o Larry, Westchester, NY, (914) 737-5004

GAY FATHERS OF GREATER PHILADELPHIA, Box 3872, Philadelphia, PA 19146, (215) 732-5400. *Meets at Gay Community Center, 222 Camac. Call for date and time.*

GAY AND BI MARRIED MEN'S GROUP, c/o Dignity, 250 South 12th Street, Philadelphia, PA 19107

GAY FATHERS, Box 13149, Philadelphia, PA 19101

GAY FATHERS COALITION, Box 1672, Newport News, VA 23601

GAY FATHERS SUPPORT GROUP, c/o Phil Herrington, P.O. Box 22744, Seattle, WA 98122

SWITCHBOARDS

ALABAMA

Birmingham
Gay Information Line
(205) 251-0682

ALASKA

Anchorage
Gay Community Center
(907) 276-3909

ARIZONA

Phoenix
Gay Help Line
(602) 251-1102

Tucson
Arizona Gay News
(602) 623-5268

ARKANSAS

Crisis Center of Arkansas Helpline
(501) 664-8834
Outside Little Rock: (800) 482-8886

CALIFORNIA

Fresno
Fresno Gay Hotline
(209) 264-HELP

Los Angeles Area
Gay and Lesbian Services Center
(213) 464-7400

Napa
Napa Gay Collective Hotline
(707) 224-3836

Oakland-Berkeley
Pacific Center
(415) 841-6224

Orange County
Gay and Lesbian Community Service Center
(714) 534-3261
(714) 859-6482

Pomona
Gay Hotline
(714) 623-1491

San Bernardino
Gay and Lesbian Community Center Hotline
(714) 824-7618

San Diego
Lesbian Gay Community Center
(619) 232-7528

San Francisco
Gay Community Center
(415) 863-9000

San Jose
Gay Community Center
(408) 293-4525
(408) 293-AGAY

Santa Barbara
Gay and Lesbian Resource Center
(805) 963-3636

Santa Rosa
(707) 544-HELP

CANADA

Calgary, Alberta
(403) 264-8973

Vancouver, British Columbia
Lesbian Information Line
(604) 734-1016

Winnipeg, Manitoba
Gays for Equality
(204) 269-8678

Halifax, Nova Scotia
Gayline
(902) 429-6969

Hamilton, Ontario
Gayline
(807) 523-7055

London, Ontario
Gayline
(807) 679-6423

Ottawa, Ontario
Gayline/Telegai
(807) 238-1717

Toronto, Ontario
Toronto Area Gays
(807) 964-6600

Montreal, Quebec Province
Gay Info—486-4404
Gayline for women: (819) 931-5330
Gayline for men: (819) 931-8668

Saskatchewan
Gayline
(306) 665-9129

COLORADO

Denver
Gay Community Center
(303) 831-6268
(303) 837-1598

Colorado Springs
Gay Hotline
(303) 471-4429

CONNECTICUT

Hartford
Gay Switchboard
(203) 522-5575

New Haven
Gay Switchboard
(203) 624-6869

DELAWARE

Gay and Lesbian Hotline
(800) 342-4012

DISTRICT OF COLUMBIA

Gay and Lesbian Switchboard
(202) 387-4348

Gay Hotline
(202) 833-3234

FLORIDA

Fort Lauderdale
Hotline
(305) 763-2857

Gainesville
Group for Gay Awareness
(904) 373-GAYS

Miami
Switchboard of Miami
(305) 358-HELP

Tampa
Gay Hotline
(813) 229-8839

Bradenton
Gay Info Line
(813) 748-5531

Orlando
Gay Community Services
(305) 843-2750

GEORGIA

Atlanta
Gay Helpline
(404) 892-0661

HAWAII

Hotline
(808) 572-1884

IDAHO

Boise
Metropolitan Community Church
(208) 342-6764

ILLINOIS

Champaign-Urbana
Gay Switchboard
(217) 384-8040

Chicago
(312) 929-HELP

INDIANA

Bloomington
Gay Lesbian Switchboard
(812) 336-GAY9

Fort Wayne
Gay/Lesbian Helpline
(219) 422-1766

Indianapolis
Gay Switchboard
(317) 546-9339

IOWA

Ames
Open Line
(515) 292-7000

Des Moines
Gay and Lesbian Coalition
(515) 279-2110

Iowa City
Gayline
(319) 353-7162

KANSAS

Wichita
Metropolitan Community Church
(316) 267-1852

KENTUCKY

Louisville
Gay/Lesbian Switchboard
(502) 637-4342

LOUISIANA

New Orleans
Gay Info Line
(504) 522-5815

MAINE

Gay Phoneline
(207) 498-6556

MARYLAND
Baltimore
Gay and Lesbian Switchboard
(301) 837-8888

MASSACHUSETTS
Amherst
Amherst Gay Hotline
(413) 545-0154
(413) 545-2645

Boston
Boston Gay Hotline
(617) 426-9371

MICHIGAN
Ann Arbor
Gay Hotline
(313) 662-1977

Detroit
Gay Lesbian Switchboard
(313) 577-3450

Lansing
Lesbian/Gay Hotline
(517) 332-1611

MINNESOTA
Minneapolis-St. Paul
Lesbian Gay Community Services
(612) 827-2821

MISSISSIPPI
Jackson
Gay Switchboard
(601) 355-7495

MISSOURI
Kansas City
GAY TALK
(816) 931-4470

St. Louis
Gay Hotline
(314) 367-0084

MONTANA
Missoula
Gay Hotlines
Men's hotline—(406) 728-8758
Women's hotline—(406) 542-2684

NEBRASKA
Lincoln
Gay Line
(402) 475-5710

Omaha
Gay Lesbian Rap Line
(402) 346-1698

NEVADA
Las Vegas
Metropolitan Community Church
(702) 642-5220

NEW HAMPSHIRE
Concord
Gay Helpline
(603) 485-5612

NEW JERSEY
New Jersey Gay Switchboard
(609) 466-1980

New Brunswick
Gay Hotline
(201) 932-7886

NEW MEXICO
Albuquerque
Common Bond
(505) 266-8041

Santa Fe
Peer Counsel
(505) 983-5598

NEW YORK

Albany
Gay Community Council
(518) 462-6138

Birmingham
Lesbian Switchboard
(607) 723-3200

Buffalo
Mattachine Society
(716) 881-5335

New York City Area
Middle Earth Switchboard
(516) 826-0600

Lesbian Switchboard
(212) 741-2610

Gay Switchboard
(212) 777-1800

Gay Hotline
(914) 948-4922

Rochester
Gay Alliance
(716) 244-8640

Syracuse
Gay Phone
(315) 423-3599

NORTH CAROLINA

Charlotte
Gay Lesbian Switchboard
(704) 525-6128

NORTH DAKOTA

Fargo
Dignity
(701) 235-7341

OHIO

Cincinnati
Gay Community Switchboard
(513) 221-7800

Cleveland
Gay Hotline
(216) 621-3380

Columbus
Gay Info-Line
OSU Gay Alliance
(614) 422-9212

Dayton
Dayton Gay Center
(evenings)
(513) 228-4875

Toledo
PRO/Toledo
(419) 243-9351

OKLAHOMA

Oklahoma City
Gay Information Line
(405) 848-7039

OREGON

Eugene
Gay and Lesbian Alliance
(503) 686-3360

Salem
Salem Hotline
(503) 399-8763

PENNSYLVANIA
Harrisburg
Gay Switchboard
(717) 234-0328

Lancaster
Gay/Lesbian Helpline
(717) 397-0691

Philadelphia
Gay Switchboard
(215) 546-7100

Pittsburgh
Gay and Lesbian Community Center
(412) 683-9422

State College
Gayline
(814) 863-0588

SOUTH CAROLINA
Charleston
Lambda
(803) 723-9419

SOUTH DAKOTA
Sioux Falls
Gay Hotline
(605) 332-4599

TENNESSEE
Memphis
Gay Switchboard
(901) 726-GAYY

Nashville
Metropolitan Community Church
(615) 320-0288

TEXAS
Austin
Gayline
(512) 477-6699

Dallas
Gayline
(214) 748-6790

San Antonio
Gay Switchboard
(512) 733-7300

UTAH
Salt Lake City
Gay Helpline
(801) 533-0927

VERMONT
Burlington
GSU Hotline
(802) 656-4173

VIRGINIA
Norfolk
Gay Information Line
(804) 625-1130

WASHINGTON
Seattle
Dorian Group
(206) 682-6044

Lesbian Resource Center
(206) 632-9631

Spokane
Gay Info Line
(509) 838-4428

WEST VIRGINIA
Charleston
Integrity
(304) 346-5106

WISCONSIN
Madison
Gay Center
(608) 257-7575

Milwaukee
Gay Hotline
(414) 562-7010

Racine
Gay Hotline
(414) 552-7331

WYOMING
Cheyenne
Gay/Lesbian Coffeehouse
(307) 637-8173

CHILDREN'S RESOURCES

CHILDREN OF GAYS
8306 Wilshire Blvd, No. 222
Beverly Hills, CA 90211
(213) 738-1008
Headquarters and hotline for national support group for kids with gay or lesbian parents. Write.

CHILDREN'S RIGHTS INC.
3443 17th Street NW
Washington, DC 20010

MOUNTAIN MEADOW COUNTRY EXPERIENCE
3736 Kenawha Street NW
Washington, DC 20015
This is a summer camp for kids of lesbian mothers (may expand to gay fathers soon).

CHILDREN OF LESBIANS AND GAYS
c/o Noel Maze
P.O. Box 12501
Fort Wayne, IN 46863

BOYS OF LESBIAN MOTHERS
953 West Broadway
Eugene, OR 97402

LEGAL RESOURCES

AMERICAN CIVIL LIBERTIES UNION, GAY RIGHTS CHAPTER, P.O. Box 480029, Los Angeles, CA 90040

LESBIAN AND GAY CENTER LEGAL AID, PROGRAM, Box 1124, San Diego, CA 92112, (619) 692-GAYS. *6–10 p.m.*

GAY RIGHTS ADVOCATES, 540 Castro Street, San Francisco, CA 94114, (415) 863-3624. *Public-interest law firm.*

LESBIAN RIGHTS PROJECT, 1370 Mission Street, 4th floor, San Francisco, CA 94103. *Outstanding legal resource; have written significant material for parents and attorneys.*

NATIONAL LAWYERS GUILD GAY CAUCUS, 558 Capp Street, San Francisco, CA 94110, (415) 285-5066. *Referrals.*

LESBIAN MOTHERS DEFENSE FUND, Box 38, Station E, Toronto, Ontario, CN M6H 4E1

GERALD A. GERASH, Attorney-at-law, 1535 Grant Street, No. 180, Denver, CO 80203, (303) 861-0700. *Specializes in legal problems of lesbians and gays.*

HOLMES, HUNTER, POLIKOFF & BODLEY, 1319 F Street NW, No. 1004, Washington, DC 20004, (202) 783-3410. *Have published articles regarding gay-custody case law. Extensive experience.*

LESBIAN AND GAY RIGHTS CAUCUS, Antioch School of Law, 2633 16th Street NW, Box 3, Washington, DC 20009, (202) 265-9500. *Contact: Gil. Legal services available.*

RIGHT TO PRIVACY FOUNDATION, 750 7th Street SE, Washington, DC 20003, (202) 546-2130. *Research, education, federal legislation.*

WOMEN'S LEGAL DEFENSE FUND, 2000 P Street NW, No. 400, Washington, DC 20036, (202) 887-0364

HEYWARD & SCHILDMEYER, Attorneys-at-law, 4834 Klondike Road, Lithonia, GA 30058, (404) 987-0455. *Specializing in gay custody, relationship contracts, wills, powers of attorney.*

RENE C. HANOVER, One North LaSalle Street, No. 1111, Chicago, IL 60602, (312) 346-9690. *Gay rights, child custody cases, relationship contracts.*

GAY AND LESBIAN ADVOCATES AND DEFENDERS, 2 Park Square, Boston, MA 02116

LESBIAN AND GAY PARENT PROJECT, 21 Bay Street, Cambridge, MA 02139, (617) 492-2655. *Advocacy and support.*

LAMBDA LEGAL DEFENSE FUND, 132 West 43rd Street, New York, NY 10036, (212) 944-9488. *They take cases relating to general gay rights (precedent-setting cases only).*

NATIONAL LAWYERS GUILD, Gay Rights Task Force, 835 Broadway, New York, NY 10003, (212) 260-1360. *Network may provide informal referrals.*

COMMUNITY LAW PROJECT, 1628 SE Ankeny Street, Portland, OR 97214, (503) 233-4747

CUSTODY ACTION FOR LESBIAN MOTHERS (CALM), Box 281, Narberth, PA 19072

ABBY ROSE RUBENFELD, Cheatham & Palermo, 43 Music

Square West, Nashville, TN 37203, (615) 244-4270. *Extensive gay practice includes custody cases.*

LESBIAN DEFENSE FUND, Box 4, Essex Junction, VT 05452, (802) 862-9046. *Fund-raising and referrals.*

GAY PARENTS LEGAL RESEARCH GROUP, Box 1723, Lynwood, WA 98036

LESBIAN MOTHERS NATIONAL DEFENSE FUND, P.O. Box 21567, Seattle, WA 98111, (206) 325-2643. *Legal, emotional, peer support for custody cases. National referrals, support. Put out "Mom's Apple Pie" newsletter.*

MOTHERS' GROUPS

LESBIAN MOTHERS GROUP, c/o Pacific Center, 2712 Telegraph Avenue, Berkeley, CA 94701, (415) 841-6224

MOTHERS AND OTHERS, 2923 Fulton, Berkeley, CA 94705, (415) 549-0755

PENINSULA MOTHERS CLUB, 444 Matadero Avenue, Palo Alto, CA 94306

LESBIAN MOTHERS GROUP, SACRAMENTO, Sacramento, CA, (916) 456-3245

LESBIAN TASK FORCE OF NOW, Box 1404, Sacramento, CA 95807, (916) 443-3470. *Support; will do fund-raisers for custody cases.*

SACRAMENTO LESBIAN MOTHERS, Sacramento, CA, (916) 966-5116

LESBIAN MOTHERS OF TEENS, San Francisco, CA, (415) 626-7109

LESBIANS WITH CHILDREN, SAN JOSE, San Jose, CA, (408) 470-9687

LESBIAN MOTHERS SUPPORT GROUP, SANTA CRUZ, Santa Cruz, CA, (408) 728-9233

LESBIAN MOTHERS SUPPORT GROUP, SANTA ROSA, Santa Rosa, CA, (707) 823-7718

LESBIAN FEMINIST MOTHERS POLITICAL ACTION, P.O. Box 65804, Station F, Vancouver, British Columbia, CN V5N 5L3

LESBIAN MOTHERS, c/o Lynn Fraser, 320 5th Avenue SE, No. 124, Calgary, CN T2G 0E5

LESBIAN MOTHERS, c/o GIRC, Box 1828, Station M, Calgary, Alberta, CN T2P 2L3, (403) 234-8973

LESBIAN MOTHERS, NEW HAVEN, P.O. Box 3438, Yale Station, New Haven, CT 06520

LESBIAN MOTHERS GROUP, BOSTON, Rubi—(617) 524-0034, Donna/Mary—(617) 298-0914, Boston, MA, (617) 524-0034

LESBIANS WITH CHILDREN, c/o Women's Educational Center, 46 Pleasant Street, Cambridge, MA 02139, (617) 354-8807

PARENTS AND CO-PARENTS RAP, c/o Daughters of Bilitis, 1151 Massachusetts Avenue, Cambridge, MA 02138, (617) 661-3633

LESBIAN MOTHERS, MARYLAND, (301) 251-1225

LESBIAN MOTHERS SUPPORT GROUP, c/o G.C.C.B., 241 West Chase Street, Baltimore, MD 21201

LESBIAN MOTHERS RAP GROUP, ST. LOUIS, St. Louis, MO, (314) 865-4623

LESBIAN MOTHERS GROUP, P.O. Box 703, Princeton, NJ 08540

DYKES AND TYKES LEGAL CUSTODY CENTER, 110 East 23rd Street, No. 502, New York, NY 10011, (212) 777-8358

LESBIAN MOTHERS SUPPORT GROUP, c/o Lesbian Resource Center, 713 Monroe Avenue, Rochester, NY 14607, (716) 244-8640

LESBIAN MOTHER SUPPORT GROUP, Cincinnati, OH, Dee—(513) 961-5934, Ginni—(513) 771-6004

LESBIAN PARENTING ALLIANCE, P.O. Box 420496, Portland, OR 97202, (503) 233-7083, (503) 224-5399

LESBIAN MOTHERS GROUP, c/o SISTERSPACE, 3500 Lancaster Avenue, Philadelphia, PA 19104, (215) 222-5110

LESBIAN MOTHERS GROUP, PAWTUCKET, P.O. Box 755, Pawtucket, RI 02860

LESBIAN MOTHERS SUPPORT GROUP—NOW, National Organization for Women (NOW), Box 40982, Memphis, TN 38104, (901) 458-1661

LESBIAN MOTHERS, HOUSTON, Houston, TX, (713) 529-4975

GAY WIVES AND MOTHERS COLLECTIVE, 57 Maide Causeway, Cambridge, England, U.K.

NORTHERN VIRGINIA LESBIAN MOTHERS GROUP, (Marilyn or Aire), (804) 734-9063

GENI MARTEL, 2105 Grove Avenue, Richmond, VA 23220, (804) 358-2939. *Lesbian mother who does counseling on child custody.*

LESBIAN AND CHILD GROUP, c/o Lois Thetford, Seattle, WA, (206) 323-0162

RESPONSIBLE GAY MOTHERS, c/o Lesbian Resource Center, 4224 University Way, Seattle, WA 98105

HEALTH SERVICES

THE SPERM BANK OF NORTHERN CALIFORNIA, Feminist Women's Health Center, 2930 McClure Street, Oakland, CA 94609. *Very open to lesbians. Equipped to ship frozen semen to other areas. Experienced.*

AIDS HOTLINE, San Francisco, CA, (415) 863-AIDS

BAY AREA PHYSICIANS FOR HUMAN RIGHTS (BAPHR), Box 14546, San Francisco, CA 94114, (415) 673-3189. *Students and doctors who support human rights and quality care for gay people.*

LYON-MARTIN CLINIC, 2480 Mission Street, San Francisco, CA 94110. *Women's health center; staff members have a lot of experience with lesbian mothers.*

MIDWIVES ALLIANCE OF NORTH AMERICA, San Francisco, CA, (415) 653-9930, Gail—(415) 653-9930—or Elizabeth—(415) 753-5997

NATIONAL GAY HEALTH FOUNDATION, Box 834, Linden Hill, NY 11354

NATIONAL GAY HEALTH EDUCATION FOUNDATION, Suite 1305, 80 Eighth Avenue, New York, NY 10011

AIDS HOTLINE, New York, NY, (212) 685-4952

FEMINIST SELF-INSEMINATION GROUP, Box 3, 190 Upper Street, London N1, England, U.K. *They have written a very informative booklet on self-insemination.*

OTHER SERVICES

PACIFIC CENTER FOR HUMAN GROWTH, 2712 Telegraph Avenue, Box 908, Berkeley, CA 94701, (415) 841-6224. *Multi-Service Counseling Center for mothers, fathers, married gays.*

ONE INC.—ONE Institute, 2256 Venice Boulevard, Los Angeles, CA 90006, (213) 735-5252. *Education, counseling, research. Largest gay library in United States. ONE Institute was founded in 1952.*

SAGE, Senior Action in a Gay Environment, Box 4071, San Diego, CA 92114. *Gay senior citizens.*

JANUS INFORMATION FACILITY, 1952 Union Street, San Francisco, CA 94123, (415) 567-0162. *Transgender resource.*

GAY PEOPLE'S UNION AT STANFORD, Old Firehouse, 2d floor, Box 8265, Stanford, CA 94305, (415) 497-1488. *At Stanford University. Have sponsored Gay Family Days for gays, kids and parents.*

WAGES DUE LESBIANS TORONTO, P.O. Box 38, Station E, Toronto, Ontario, CN M6H 4E2. *Political organization, very supportive to lesbian mothers.*

NATIONAL ORGANIZATION FOR WOMEN (NOW), 425 13th Street NW, No. 1001, Washington, DC 20004. *Some local chapters of NOW have lesbian mothers' support groups; write.*

PRAIRIE CALF, 802 West Illinois, No. 1, Urbana, IL 61801, (217) 359-6359. *Local referrals; possibly loans for local mothers in custody cases.*

NORTH SUBURBAN GAY ASSOCIATION, Box 465, Wilmette, IL 60091, (312) 475-6934. *Membership includes married gays.*

THE LOVING BROTHERHOOD, Journal for Personal Transformation, Box 556GY, Sussex, NJ 07461, (201) 875-4710. *International spiritual support group has many parents—Correspondents.*

WAGES DUE LESBIANS, P.O. Box 326, Brooklyn, NY 11215. *Politically oriented organization, very supportive of lesbian mothers; write.*

DISABLED LESBIAN ALLIANCE, R.D. 1, Box 98, Monticello,

NY 12701, (914) 794-6121. *Many disabled lesbians are mothers too and need and deserve support!*

NATIONAL GAY TASK FORCE, 80 Fifth Avenue, New York, NY 10011, (212) 741-5800

WAGES DUE LESBIANS LONDON, 20 Staverton Road, London, NW 2, England U.K. *Political organization, very supportive on lesbian mother issues.*

FILMS

CHOOSING CHILDREN; CAMBRIDGE DOCUMENTARY FILMS, P.O. Box 385, Cambridge, MA 02139, (617) 354-3677. *Outstanding film about lesbians becoming parents.*

IN THE BEST INTERESTS OF THE CHILDREN; IRIS FILMS, Box 5353, Berkeley, CA 94705. *Film by and about lesbian mothers, 16 mm color available for sale or rental.*

SANDY AND MADELEINE'S FAMILY; MULTI-MEDIA RESOURCE CENTER, Box 439E, San Francisco, CA 94102. *Thirty-minute documentary film about a family with lesbian parents.*

PERIODICALS

LESBIAN MOTHERS NETWORKER, c/o Pacific Center for Human Growth, P.O. Box 908, Berkeley, CA 94701, (415) 841-6224

L.A. COMMUNITY YELLOW PAGES, 1314 South Tremaine Street, Los Angeles, CA 90019, (213) 939-1200. *Annual directory of businesses and resources serving Southern California's gay community.*

WOMEN'S YELLOW PAGES, Box 66093, Los Angeles, CA 90066

GAY AREA PRIVATE TELEPHONE DIRECTORY, Box 14752, San Francisco, CA 94114, (415) 861-3905. *Local directory for individuals, services and businesses.*

NURTURING NEWS, 187 Caselli Avenue, San Francisco, CA 94114. *Not specifically gay; newsletter for "nurturing men."*

NATIONAL WOMEN'S INFORMATION EXCHANGE, 1195 Valencia Street, San Francisco, CA 94110, (415) 824-6800. *Organizational mailing lists available.*

CAPITOL REGION CONFERENCE OF CHURCHES, 30 Arbor Street, Hartford, CT 06106, (203) 236-1295. *Publishes* Directory of Resources *for lesbians and gay men, transvestites and transsexuals.*

MEN & WIFE NEWSLETTER, c/o P. G. Springer, Box 2505A, Champaign, IL 61820

REVIEW, Box 7195, Westchester, IL 60153, (312) 620-6946. *6–11 p.m. For bi and gay married men.*

GAIA'S GUIDE for Gay Women, 132 West 24th Street, New York, NY 10011. *Resource guide for the United States, Canada, Western Europe; $10 mail order.*

GAYELLOW PAGES, Renaissance House, Box 292, Village Station, New York, NY 10014, (212) 929-7720. *National listing of services and organizations. Update due in 1985.*

JOURNAL OF HOMOSEXUALITY, c/o Haworth Press, 149 Fifth Avenue, New York, NY 10010, (212) 228-2800. *Research journal; they have published papers on gay and lesbian parenting.*

TASK FORCE REPORT, National Gay Task Force, 80 Fifth Avenue, New York, NY 10011, (212) 741-5800

WOMEN HELPING WOMEN DIRECTORY, Women's Action Alliance, 370 Lexington Avenue, New York, NY 10017, (212) 532-8330. *A state-by-state directory of services, $14.95.*

GAY BIBLIOGRAPHY, Gay Task Force, American Library Association, Box 2383, Philadelphia, PA 19103, (215) 471-3322. *$1.50 prepaid; send SASE for complete info.*

MEMPHIS GAY COALITION, LOCAL GAY SERVICES DIRECTORY, Box 3038, Memphis, TN 38103. *Men's and women's support groups.*

MOM'S APPLE PIE, c/o Lesbian Mothers National Defense Fund, P.O. Box 21537, Seattle, WA 98111

RELIGIOUS ORGANIZATIONS

AMERICAN BAPTISTS CONCERNED, 2418 Browning Street, Berkeley, CA 94702

AXIOS, Eastern and Orthodox Christians, Box 3361, Beverly Hills, CA 90212

UNITED LESBIAN AND GAY CHRISTIAN SCIENTISTS, Box 7467, Beverly Hills, CA 90211, (213) 656-9623

AFFIRMATION, Gay and Lesbian Mormons, Box 46022, Los Angeles, CA 90046

LUTHERANS CONCERNED, Box 19114A, Los Angeles, CA 90019, (213) 663-7816. *Counseling, speakers bureau, worship.*

METROPOLITAN COMMUNITY CHURCHES UNIVERSAL FELLOWSHIP, 5300 Santa Monica Boulevard, Los Angeles, CA 90029, (213) 464-5100. *National fellowship with many local churches, some of which sponsor parents' groups.*

AFFIRMATION, Gay and Lesbian Mormons, Box 26302, San Francisco, CA 94126, (415) 685-1674

ORION FELLOWSHIP ALLIANCE, Box 4768, San Francisco, CA 94101, (415) 921-1662. *Seventh-Day Adventists.*

UNITARIAN UNIVERSALIST GAY CAUCUS, 258 Edgewood Avenue, San Francisco, CA 94117, (415) 731-6437

UNITED CHURCH COALITION FOR LESBIAN/GAY CONCERNS, Box 1926, San Francisco, CA 94101, (415) 540-0751

COUNCIL ON HOMOSEXUALITY AND RELIGION, Box 1912, Winnipeg, Manitoba, CN R3C 3R2

AFFIRM, United Church of Canada caucus, c/o 3521 University St., Montreal, Quebec, CN H3A 2A9

CHURCH OF GOD, Caucus for Gays and Lesbians, P.O. Box 9163, Denver, CO 80209

BRETHREN/MENNONITE COUNCIL FOR GAY CONCERNS, Box 24060, Washington, DC 20024

DIGNITY INC., 1500 Massachusetts Avenue, No. 11, Washington, DC 20005, (202) 861-0017. *National organization of gay Catholics. Some local chapters sponsor parents' groups.*

INTEGRITY INTERNATIONAL, 4550 Connecticut Avenue NW, No. 605, Washington, DC 20008, (202) 362-0440. *National organization of gay Episcopalians.*

UNITED METHODISTS FOR LESBIAN AND GAY CONCERNS, Box 1021, Evanston, IL 60204

UNITARIAN UNIVERSALIST OFFICE OF LESBIAN/GAY CONCERNS, 25 Beacon Street, Boston, MA 02108, (617) 742-2100. *Education, programming, counseling and ceremonial services.*

NEW WAYS MINISTRY, Catholic Advocacy Group, 4012 29th Street, Mount Rainier, MD 20712

PASSIONISTS, Southern Baptists, Box 346, Pasadena, MD 21122

PRESBYTERIANS FOR LESBIAN/GAY CONCERNS, R.D. 1, Box 356, Hampton, NJ 08827, (201) 735-9714

GAY PEOPLE IN CHRISTIAN SCIENCE, 15 Christopher Street, New York, NY 10014

HUMAN SEXUALITY OFFICE, National Council of Churches, 475 Riverside Drive, No. 711, New York, NY 10115

INTERNATIONAL CONFERENCE OF GAY AND LESBIAN JEWS, Box 1270, New York, NY 10116

FRIENDS COMMITTEE ON GAY CONCERNS, Box 222, Sumneytown, PA 18084, (215) 234-8424. *Gay Friends (Quakers).*

JEHOVAH'S WITNESSES GAY SUPPORT GROUP, Box 3744, St. Thomas, VI 00801, (809) 775-2640. *Strictest confidence; SASE.*

SUPPORT GROUPS FOR FAMILIES

PARENTS AND FRIENDS OF LESBIANS AND GAYS, P.O. Box 24565, Los Angeles, CA 90024, (213) 472-8952. *Support groups nationwide for families—including kids. Write for local referrals.*

SPOUSES OF GAYS, 450 Sutter Street, No. 2100, San Francisco, CA 94109

PARENTS OF GAYS MISSISSAUGA, c/o 3323 Kings Mastings Crest, Mississauga, Ontario, CN L5L 1G5

SPOUSES OF GAYS, c/o Caryn Miller, 206 St. Clair Avenue West, Toronto, Ontario, CN M4V 1R2

PARENTS OF GAYS, Box 9094, Ottawa, Ontario, CN K1G 3T8

NATIONAL FEDERATION OF PARENTS AND FRIENDS OF GAYS, 5715 16th Street NW, Washington, DC 20011, (202) 726-3223. *May also give kids a chance to meet others. Call or write for local chapter referral.*

SIGMA (SPOUSES IN A GAY MARRIAGE), P.O. Box 262, Pella, IA 50219. *Use only initials on envelopes, please!*

STRAIGHT PARTNERS, P.O. Box 943, Addison, IL 60101

STRAIGHT PARTNERS—SPOUSES ANONYMOUS, P.O. Box 6191, South Bend, IN 46660

STRAIGHT PARTNERS, Box 1603, Hyattsville, MD 20788

FAMILIES AND FRIENDS OF GAYS OF ROCHESTER, Box 601, Fairport, NY 14405, (716) 266-1247

PARENTS OF LESBIANS AND GAY MEN, P.O. Box 553, Lenox Hill Station, New York, NY 10021, (914) 793-5198

GAY-STRAIGHT PARTNERS ALLIANCE, 810 East 29th Street, Eugene, OR 97405

SPOUSES OF GAYS, Philadelphia, PA, (215) 288-6959

FAMILIES AND FRIENDS OF GAYS AND LESBIANS, 5336 Northeast 184th, Seattle, WA 98155, (206) 363-2762

SPOUSES OF GAYS, 2319 West McKinley Boulevard, Milwaukee, WI 53205

APPENDIX TWO

Bibliographies

The number of articles and professional studies about lesbian and gay parenting is constantly growing. Additionally, the body of legal material and case documentation is increasing as more gay fathers and lesbian mothers take the fight for their parental rights into the courtrooms.

If you are unable to locate some of the listed articles at your local library, the Bay Area Gay Fathers (P.O. Box 31622, San Francisco, CA 94131) maintains an extensive archive of materials, including articles on married gays and family issues. For a nominal fee, they will send copies of material in their library and an up-to-date bibliography. Please send SASE with your inquiry.

BOOKS OF SPECIFIC INTEREST TO PARENTS

Achtenberg, Roberta (ed.), *Sexual Orientation and the Law,* New York, Boardman, 1985.

Anti-Sexism Committee, National Lawyers Guild, *A Gay Parent's Legal Guide to Child Custody,* National Lawyers Guild, 1982. Very useful booklet; gives information on what to expect, what to do and where to turn during custody dispute. Available through National Lawyers' Guild, 558 Capp Street, San Francisco, CA 94110.

Bell, A. P., and Weinberg, M. S., *Homosexualities: A Study of Diversities Among Men and Women,* New York, Simon and Schuster, 1978.

Berzon, B., and Leighton, R. (eds.), *Positively Gay,* Millbrae, California, Celestial Arts, 1979. Anthology with pieces on parenting.

Borhek, M., *Coming Out to Parents: A Two-Way Survival Guide for Lesbians and Gay Men and Their Families,* New York, Pilgrim Press, 1983.

Bosche, Suzanne, *Jenny Lives with Eric and Martin,* translated from the Danish by Louis Mackay, Gay Men's Press, 1983, P.O. Box 247, London N15 6RW. Wonderful photostory for children of gay parents about Jenny, who lives with her dad and his lover. Warm.

Brown, Howard, *Familiar Faces, Hidden Lives: The Story of Homosexual Men in America Today,* New York, Harcourt Brace Jovanovich, 1976.

Clark, Don, *Living Gay,* Millbrae, California, Celestial Arts, 1979.

———, *Loving Someone Gay,* Millbrae, California, Celestial Arts, 1977.

Curry, Hayden, and Clifford, Denis, *A Legal Guide for Lesbian and Gay Couples,* Nolo Press, 1980. Outstanding resource for all lesbian and gay couples; includes information on custody and parent's and partner's rights. Highly recommended.

Cutter, Wendy Judith; Sayyed, Yasmin A.; and Vaughn, Jeane, *Lesbian Parenting Child Custody Struggles: Community Organizing and Legal Defense Networks,* privately printed, 1982. Available from Susan Parker Defense Committee, 524C Ocean View Avenue, Santa Cruz, CA 95062.

Fairchild, B., and Hayward, N., *Now That You Know: What Every Parent Should Know About Homosexuality,* New York, Harcourt Brace Jovanovich, 1979.

Feminist Self-Insemination Group, *Self-Insemination,* privately printed, 1984. Written by a lesbian feminist group in London; some of the references are distinctly British. This is, however, a valuable book which examines the social, political and emotional aspects of parenting. Write Box 3, 190 Upper Street, London N1, U.K.

Gantz, Joe, *Whose Child Cries: Children of Gay Parents Talk About Their Lives,* Jalmar Press, 1983.

Gay Fathers of Toronto, *Gay Fathers: Some of Their Stories, Experience and Advice,* privately printed, 1981.

Gibson, G. G., with Mary Jo Risher, *By Her Own Admission: A Lesbian Mother's Fight to Keep Her Son,* Garden City, N.Y., Doubleday & Company, Inc., 1977.

Hanscombe, Gillian E., and Forster, Jackie, *Rocking the Cradle: Lesbian Mothers—A Challenge in Family Living,* Allyson Pub., Boston, 1982.

Hitchens, Donna J., J.D., *Lesbian Mother Litigation Manual,* Lesbian Rights Project, 1982. Geared toward the attorney preparing for custody litigation, this is an outstanding resource by a top-notch attorney. It may be rather dense for the layperson unfamiliar with legalese. *Highly recommended.* Write Lesbian Rights Project, 1370 Mission Street, 4th floor, San Francisco, CA 94103.

Jay, Karla, and Young, Allen (eds.), *After You're Out: Personal Experiences of Gay Men and Lesbian Women,* New York, Links Books, 1975. Anthology with essays by a lesbian mother and a gay father. Social/political orientation.

Jullion, Jeanne, *Long Way Home: The Odyssey of a Lesbian Mother and Her Children,* San Francisco/Pittsburgh, Cleio Press, 1985.

Lesbian Rights Project—San Francisco, *Lesbian Mothers and Their Children: Annotated Bibliography of Legal and Psychological Materials* 1983. Oriented toward preparation of legal cases, this bibliography includes legal materials with summaries, psychological materials and other miscellany. Write Lesbian Rights Project, 1370 Mission Street, 4th floor, San Francisco, CA 94103.

Macklin, E., and Rubin, R. (eds.), *Contemporary Families and Alternative Lifestyles,* Beverly Hills, Sage Publications, 1983.

Martin, Del, and Lyon, Phyllis, "Lesbians Are Mothers Too," from *Lesbian/Woman,* San Francisco, Glide Publications, 1972.

McWhirter, D., and Mattison, A., *The Male Couple: How Relationships Develop,* Englewood Cliffs, N.J., Prentice-Hall, 1984. Extensive, up-to-date research on gay male couples, their experience, attitudes, life-styles. Section relating to children examines primarily the effects of one partner's having children on the overall relationship. *Highly recommended.*

Mendola, Mary, *The Mendola Report: A New Look at Gay Couples in America,* New York, Crown Publishers, 1980. Primarily anecdotal, this book presents interviews with many couples and individuals. When children are significant to the relationship, their input and feedback is included as well as the parents' analysis of the children's effects.

Moses, A. Elfin, and Haekins, Robert O., "Gay Parents," from *Counseling Lesbian Women and Gay Men—A Life Issues Approach,* St. Louis, C. V. Mosby Co., 1982.

National Gay Task Force, Gay Parents' Support Packet, National Gay Task Force, 1983. Resources, articles, letters by professionals, this packet contains a variety of useful information. Available from the National Gay Task Force, 80 Fifth Ave., New York, NY 10011, $4.00.

Pies, Cheri, *Lesbians Choosing Children: A Workbook,* Berkeley, Calif., Spinsters, Inc., 1985.

Rofes, Eric, "Loving Your Gay Parent," in *The Kids' Book of Divorce,* Lewis Publishing Co., 1981.

Severance, Jane, *When Megan Went Away,* Lollipop Power, Inc. Fiction.

Taylor, Sheila Ortiz, *Faultlines,* Naiad Press, 1982. Fiction.

Vida, Ginny (ed.), *Our Right to Love: A Lesbian Resource Book,* Englewood Cliffs, N.J., Prentice-Hall, Inc., 1978. "Sharing Your Lesbian Lifestyle with Your Children." Also national resource listings.

Wyland, Francie, *Motherhood, Lesbianism and Child Custody,* Wages Due Lesbians and Falling Wall Press, 1977. Primarily a social and political treatise.

OTHER BOOKS OF INTEREST

Farrell, W., *The Liberated Man: Beyond Masculinity: Freeing Men and Their Relationships with Women,* New York, Random House, 1974.

Green, R., *Sexual Identity Conflict in Children and Adults,* New York, Penguin Books, 1975.

Hope, Karol, and Young, Nancy, *Momma: A Sourcebook for Single Mothers,* New York, New American Library, 1976.

Jay, Karla, and Young, Allen, *The Gay Report: Lesbians and Gay Men Speak Out About Sexual Experiences and Lifestyles,* New York, Summit Books, 1979.

Jones, C. R., *Understanding Gay Relatives and Friends,* Somers, Conn., Seabury Press, 1978.

Katz, J., *Gay American History,* New York, Thomas Y. Crowell Company, 1976.

Kinsey, A. C., Pomeroy, W. B., and Martin, C., *Sexual Behavior in the Human Male,* Philadelphia, W. B. Saunders, 1948.

Kinsey, A. C., Pomeroy, W. B., et al., *Sexual Behavior in the Human Female,* Philadelphia, W. B. Saunders, 1953.

Klein, Fred, *The Bisexual Option: A Concept of One-Hundred Per Cent Intimacy,* New York, Arbor House, 1978.

Klinman, D., and Kohl, R., *Fatherhood U.S.A.,* Garland Publishing, 1984. The first national guide to programs, services and resources for and about fathers.

Marmor, Judd (ed.), *Homosexual Behavior: A Modern Reappraisal,* New York, Basic Books, 1980.

Masters, W. H., and Johnson, V. E., *Homosexuality in Perspective,* Boston: Little, Brown, 1979.

Nahas, R., and Turley, M., *The New Couple: Women and Gay Men,* New York, Seaview Books, 1980.

O'Neill, N., and O'Neill, G., *Open Marriage,* New York, Avon Books, 1972.

Paul, Weinrich, Gonsiorek & Hotvedt (eds.), *Homosexuality: Social, Psychological and Biological Issues,* Beverly Hills, Sage Publications, 1982.

Piaget, J., *The Language and Thought of the Child* (3d ed.), London, Routledge & Kegan Paul, 1959.

Pogrebin, Letty Cottin, *Growing Up Free: Raising Your Child in the Eighties,* New York, McGraw-Hill, 1980.

Silverstein, Charles, *A Family Matter: A Parents' Guide to Homosexuality,* New York, McGraw-Hill, 1977.

Spock, Benjamin, M.D., *Baby and Child Care,* New York, Pocket Books, 1946.

Tripp, C. A., *The Homosexual Matrix,* New York, McGraw-Hill, 1975.

Weinberg, G., *Society and the Healthy Homosexual,* New York, St. Martin's Press, 1972.

Weinberg, M. S., and Williams, C. J., *Male Homosexuals: Their Problems and Adaptations,* New York, Oxford University Press, 1974.

Weinberg, Martin S., and Bell, Alan P., *Homosexuality: An Annotated Bibliography,* New York, Harper & Row, 1972.

ARTICLES AND PROFESSIONAL PAPERS

Ager, Susan, "Gay Parenting: Can Love Conquer All?," San Jose *Mercury-News,* November 28, 1982.

Armanno, Benna F., "The Lesbian Mother: Her Right to Child Custody," 4 *Golden Gate Law Review* 1, 1973.

Arthur, C., M.D., and English, K., "An Expert Testifies in a Lesbian Parenting Child Custody Case," Portland, Oregon, Community Law Project. Write: Community Law Project, 1628 Southeast Ankeny Street, Portland, OR 97214.

Barnet, Alison, "Lesbians Choosing Children," *Bay Windows* (Boston), Vol. 2, No. 1 (January 5–18, 1984).

Basile, R. A., "Lesbian Mothers I" 2 *Womens Rights Law Reporter* 3, 1974.

Bozett, Frederick W., "Gay Fathers: Evolution of the Gay-Father Identity," *American Journal of Orthopsychiatry,* Vol. 51, No. 3 (July 1981).

———, "Gay Fathers: How and Why They Disclose Their Homosexuality to Their Children," *Family Relations,* Vol. 29, No. 2 (April 1980).

———, "Gay Fathers—Identity Conflict Resolution Through Integrative Sanctioning," *Alternative Lifestyles,* Vol. 4, No. 1 (February 1981).

Clark, Jill, "Gay Father Appeals Loss of Visiting Rights," *Gay Community News,* July 31, 1982.

Clemmons, Nelda, "Daddies' Group Has Some Friends," Tampa *Times,* August 28, 1980.

Coleman, E., "Developmental Stages of the Coming Out Process," *Journal of Homosexuality,* 7 (2–3) (1982).

Copeland, D., "What It Feels Like to Be the Walking Talking Son of a Bisexual Mother," *Christopher Street,* 2 (11) (May 1978).

Crittenden, Danielle, "Dad Left Mom for a Man," Toronto *Sun,* July 25, 1982.

Cummings, Judith, "A Gay's Fight to Become a Father," San Francisco *Chronicle,* January 19, 1983.

———, "Homosexual Views Adoption Approval as Victory," New York *Times,* January 10, 1983.

Devine, Andrea, "CLUM Supports Rights of Lesbian Parents," Civil Liberties Union of Massachusetts, *The Docket,* Vol. 13, No. 3 (August 1983).

Dolce, Joe, "Gay Daddies Shatter Stereotypes," *The Advocate,* January 6, 1983.

Dorman, Michael, "Father Knows Best," *Christopher Street,* Vol. 7, No. 3.

Dormont, Paul, M.D., "The Homosexual Parent," *Sexual Medicine Today,* (October 1978).

Eiduson, B., and Alexander, J., "The Role of Children in Alternative Family Styles," *Journal of Social Issues,* No. 34 (1978).

Elias, Marilyn, "Are Gays Fit Parents?," San Francisco *Chronicle,* September 3, 1979.

Epstein, Renee, "Children of Gays," *Christopher Street,* June 1979.

Fadiman, Anne, "The Double Closet: How Two Gay Fathers Deal with Their Children and Ex-Wives," *Life,* Vol. 6, No. 5 (May 1983).

Fitzgerald, John, "When a Parent Is Homosexual," Toronto *Globe & Mail,* January 5, 1984.

Franks, Lucinda, "Teens Who Have Gay Parents," San Francisco *Chronicle,* May 30, 1974.

Garett, Thomas, "The Pain and Pride of Gay Fathers," *New York Native,* No. 25 (November 16–29, 1981).

Gay Fathers Coalition, "So You're a Gay Father," P.O. Box 50360, Washington, D.C. 20004

———, "It's Catch-22 for Gay Parents," *Gay News,* No. 110 (January 13–26, 1977).

———, "Just Joel & Me & Baby Makes Three," *Gay News,* No. 237 (April 1–14, 1982).

Gengle, Dean, "All in the Gay Family," *The Advocate,* September 1977.

———, "Gay Fathers Unlimited: A Solution for Some," *The Advocate,* October 22, 1975.

Giteck, Lenny, "Gay Parents in Profile," *The Advocate,* June 1979.

Goodman, Bernice, "The Lesbian Mother," *American Journal of Orthopsychiatry,* Vol. 43, (1973).

Goodman, Ellen, "Homosexuality of a Parent: A New Issue in Custody Disputes," 5 *Monash University Law Review* 305, 1979.

Graham, Steve, "Life as a Gay Father," *Out and Out,* (Berkeley), Vol. 1, No. 8.

Grant, Greg, "Gay Parents as Custodians or Custody Seekers," Department of Human Relations, University of Oklahoma, July 1979.

Green, Richard, "Sexual Identity of 37 Children Raised by Homosexual or Transsexual Parents," *American Journal of Psychiatry,* Vol. 135, 1978.

Gunther, Catherine, "Gay Dads and Gay Moms: The Parents Are Alright," *City Paper,* Baltimore, July 13, 1979.

Harris, Barbara S., "Lesbian Mother Child Custody: Legal and Psychiatric Aspects," *Bulletin of the American Academy of Psychology and Law,* Vol. 5, No. 75 (1977).

Harry, J., "The Marital Liaisons of Gay Men," *Family Coordinator,* 28, 622–629, 1979.

Hart, H. (chairperson), *Families and Children of Gays,* Final Report of the Task Force on Sexual Preference, State of Oregon Department of Human Resources, 1978.

Hippler, Mike, "Absentee Fathers," *Bay Area Reporter,* March 10, 1983.

Hitchens, D. J., Martin, D., and Morgan, M., "An Alternative View to Child Custody When One Parent Is a Homosexual," 17 *Conciliation Courts Review* 27 (December 1979).

Hitchens, Donna J., J.D., "Social Attitudes, Legal Standards and Personal Trauma in Child Custody Cases," *Journal of Homosexuality,* Vol. 5, Nos. 1–2, 1979.

Hoeffer, Beverly, "Children's Acquisition of Sex-Role Behavior in Lesbian Mother Families," *American Journal of Orthopsychiatry,* Vol. 43, 1983.

Hunter, N. D., and Polikoff, N. D., "Custody Rights of Lesbian Mothers: Legal Theory and Litigation Strategy," 25 *Buffalo Law Review* 691, 1976.

Kirkpatrick, M., Roy, R., and Smith, K., "A New Look at Lesbian Mothers," *Human Behavior,* Vol. 5, No. 8 (August 1976).

Kirkpatrick, M., Smith, C., and Roy, R., "Lesbian Mothers and Their Children: A Comparative Study," *American Journal of Orthopsychiatry,* Vol. 43 (July 1981).

Klaitch, Dolores, "Parents Who Are Gay," *New Times,* July 1976.

Larkin, Mary Ann, "Coping Alone: Gay Parents and Children," *The Hill Rag,* Washington, D.C., April 1, 1980.

Latham, "Tender Mournings: Progress of a Faggot Father," *Gay Sunshine Press,* Summer/Fall 1979.

Lewin, Ellen, "Lesbianism and Motherhood: Implications for Child Custody, *Human Organization,* Vol. 40, No. 1 (1981).

———, and Lyons, Terrie, "Lesbians and Heterosexual Mothers," Paper for the American Psychological Association, September 1979.

Linscott, Gillian, "Lesbian Mother Wins Custody of Twins," *The Guardian,* November 5, 1976.

Lippincott, Robin, "Father Awarded Custody of Two Children," *Gay Community News,* October 6, 1979.

Loshak, David, "Ban on Artificial Insemination for Lesbians Rejected," London *Daily Telegraph,* June 27, 1978.

Lynch, Michael, "Forgotten Fathers," *The Body Politic,* April 1978.

MacAdams, Lewis, "Kramer vs. Kramer with a Twist," *L.A. Weekly,* November 26–December 2, 1982.

Maddox, Brenda, "Homosexual Parents," *Psychology Today,* February 1982.

Mahon, Steve, "Gay Love Is a Family Affair," *Bay Area Reporter,* October 21, 1982.

Mayadas, N., and Duehn, W., "Children in Gay Families: An

Investigation of Services," *Homosexual Counseling Journal,* Vol. 3, No. 2 (1976).

Mehren, Elizabeth, "Lesbian Mothers: Two New Studies Shatter Stereotypes," Los Angeles *Times,* June 1, 1983.

Miller, Brian, "Gay Fathers and Their Children, *The Family Coordinator,* Vol. 28, No. 4 (October 1979).

Miller, Brian, Ph.D., "Unpromised Paternity: The Life-Style of Gay Fathers," in M. P. Levin (ed.), *Gay Men,* New York, Harper & Row, 1979.

Miller, J., Jacobsen, R., and Bigner, J., "The Child's Home Environment for Lesbian Versus Heterosexual Mothers," *Journal of Homosexuality,* No. 7 (1981).

Morin, S., and Schultz, S., "The Gay Movement and the Rights of Children," *Journal of Social Issues,* Vol. 34, No. 2 (1978).

Morrison, Cheryl, "When Gays Are Parents," *Blueboy,* September 1979.

Mulroy, Brad, "Life for a Gay Father," *New York City News,* November 17, 1982.

Mungo, Raymond, "When They Come to Take Your Child Away," *Christopher Street,* April 1977.

Nash, Phil, "Families with Gay Fathers," *Westwood,* November 4, 1982.

———, "Gay Dads Speak Out," *Out Front* (Denver), Vol. 7, No. 15 (October 15, 1982).

———, "Life as a Gay Father," *Nurturing News,* September 1982.

Osman, Shelomo, "My Stepfather Is a She," *Family Process,* Vol. 11, 1972.

Pagelow, Mildred, "Lesbian Mothers," Paper for American Sociological Association meeting, New York, 1976.

Perry, James W., "Coming Out: I'm Out, 33, and a Father," *Gay Community News* (Boston), February 28, 1981.

Pogrebin, Letty Cottin, "The Secret Fear That Keeps Us from Raising Free Children," *Ms.,* October 1980.

Rees, Richard L., "A Comparison of Children of Lesbian and Single Heterosexual Mothers on Three Measures of Socialization," Dissertation Abstracts International, 1979.

Riddle, D. I., "Relating to Children: Gays as Role Models," *Journal of Social Issues,* Vol. 34, No. 3 (1978).

Riley, Marlyn, "The Avowed Lesbian Mother and Her Right to Child Custody," *San Diego Law Review,* Vol. 12, 1975.

Risemberg, Lee, "Children of Gays," *Frontiers,* Vol. 1, No. 15 (November 25–December 9, 1982).

Rivera, Rhonda R., "Our Straight-Laced Judges: The Legal Position of Homosexual Persons in the United States," 30 *Hastings Law Journal* 799, 1979.

Rock, Maxine, "A Very Private Torment," Atlanta (March 1979).

Schultz, Mark, "Expanding the Parent Pool: Adoption and Gay Men Who Wish to Father," *The Advocate,* July 21, 1983.

Sher, Mike, "Special Custody Problems Affecting Gays," *The Village Voice,* February 26, 1982.

Shipp, E. R., "A Lesbian Who Won a Child Custody Battle," New York *Times,* September 5, 1980.

Smith, Emilie, "My Father the Fluff: Coming Out from a Daughter's Perspective," *The Advocate,* July 21, 1983.

Stambolian, George, "Father Courage," *Christopher Street,* Issue 68.

Stephens, Mark, "A Minority Within a Minority," *Nurturing News,* Vol. 4, No. 3 (September 1982).

Stewart, Pearl, "Lesbian's Suit for Visiting Rights," San Francisco *Chronicle,* April 23, 1983.

Sutton, Stuart, "The Lesbian Family: Rights in Conflict under the Uniform Parentage Act," 10 *Golden Gate Law Review* 1007, 1980.

Vecsey, George, "Approval Given for Homosexual to Adopt a Boy," New York *Times,* June 21, 1979.

Voeller, Bruce, and Walters, James, "Gay Fathers," *The Family Coordinator,* April 1978.

Weeks, R., Derdyn, A. P., and Langman, M., "Two Cases of Children of Homosexuals," Paper, American Association, Psychiatric Services for Children, 1975.

Welty, Alan, "Gay Fathering: Unique Problems, Unique Approaches," *Out Front* (Denver), Vol. 8, No. 9 (July 22, 1983).

Woods, Charles, "Growing Pains," *Nurturing News,* Vol. 4, No. 3 (September 1982).

Zemel, Sue, "Choosing to Parent," *The Advocate,* April 30, 1981.

Index